THE
BLACK
AGENDA

THE
BLACK
AGENDA

BOLD SOLUTIONS
FOR A BROKEN SYSTEM

■ ■ ■

EDITED BY **Anna Gifty Opoku-Agyeman**

FOREWORD BY **Tressie McMillan Cottom**

St. Martin's Press
New York

First published in the United States by St. Martin's Press, an imprint of St. Martin's Publishing Group

www.stmartins.com

Library of Congress Cataloging-in-Publication Data

Names: Opoku-Agyeman, Anna Gifty, editor. | McMillan Cottom, Tressie, writer of foreword.
Title: The black agenda: bold solutions for a broken system / edited by Anna Gifty Opoku-Agyeman; foreword by Tressie McMillan Cottom.
Description: First edition. | New York: St. Martin's Press, 2022. | Includes bibliographical references.
Identifiers: LCCN 2021048592 | ISBN 9781250276872 (hardcover) | ISBN 9781250276889 (ebook)
Subjects: LCSH: African Americans—Social conditions—1975– | Blacks—Social conditions—United States—21st century. | African Americans—Civil rights. | Anti-racism—United States. | United States—Social policy—1993– | Social change—United States.
Classification: LCC E185.86 .B52365 2022 | DDC 305.896/073—dc23/eng/20211019
LC record available at https://lccn.loc.gov/2021048592

Our books may be purchased in bulk for promotional, educational, or business use. Please contact your local bookseller or the Macmillan Corporate and Premium Sales Department at 1-800-221-7945, extension 5442, or by email at MacmillanSpecialMarkets@macmillan.com.

First Edition: 2022

10   9   8   7   6   5   4   3   2   1

WHAT'S ON THE AGENDA?

FOREWORD
Dr. Tressie McMillan Cottom

No matter where you show up on the spectrum of Blackness, the United States owes you something. And it's clear that a significant part of the story of Black freedom and Black revolutionary thought rests upon the United States' social contract with its citizens. In the U.S., the tension in the social contract has always come down to recognizing the full citizenship of Black people across our heterogeneous exposure to this country. But what's been made abundantly clear is that regardless of how Black people got here, the social contract has only ever been extended to us on extractive terms.

When we think about the relationship between racism, capitalism, and the debt owed, we need to talk about how debt has shaped and does continue to shape: 1) how Black people can leverage the full expression of our citizenship and the full franchise; and 2) how debt operates in our individual and collective lives. There is no progress or progressive agenda to me unless that debt, in all its forms, is fully understood and agreed to by all parties.

Which brings us to 2020, a year marked by the effect that technologies have had on our social and democratic institutions as well as public life. A moment where the divides that have so determined the boundaries of academic discourse were relitigated. What people may not understand is that for

Black scholars, this reality of engaging with the public across different types of institutions has always been true. As the late W. E. B. Du Bois said, Black scholars just don't have the luxury of not having themselves and their work enmeshed in public discourse, public life, and social commentary. And I have always believed this to not just be true but also essential to how Black scholars understand their work. In 2020, I think other people began noting our lived reality as well.

Black expertise is, in many ways, an attempt to wed one's lived experience and personal narrative to empirical realities in direct response to the resistance on the part of gatekeepers, especially those that can only hear empirical expertise. What I have known is that gatekeepers are fundamentally distrustful of Black subjects as unassailable authors of our own stories. Black experts are viewed as counter storytellers, the counter narrative, and instead of coming to us with the exact same questions posed to our white counterparts, they confine us to so-called race talk.

The truth is no one wants a meritocracy more than Black people. Despite our attempts to elevate our earned status to override our inherited status, we embody a lower status due to race and/or class. Whiteness needs us. The body politic needs us. It is not going to make it without our perspectives, without these forms of expertise, which means that the next frontier of honoring Black expertise should be more than just increasing representation and diversity of voices in the room.

History has made clear that Black people don't need to learn how to find the practical significance of our work, but we do need to move that to the center, and that's what this book does—it moves us to the center. When you move the conversations about Black lives and Black experiences as well as anti-

Blackness, racism, inequality, and equity into the center, it is literally better for everyone. We become better. Our policy is better. Our inferences are better. Our conclusions are better, stronger, and more defensible. The evidence, both qualitative and quantitative, is clear: the quality of debate diminishes when you ignore diversity.

Decentering Black voices is what some may call "erasure," one of those theory words that no one has defined well publicly. And the way erasure shows up for Black experts, especially Black women, is hypervisibility and silencing. Having more Black people in the room without extending them the commensurate status and power and resources that would have come with that position had they been a man and/or been white is erasure. And simply refusing to include us in spaces is also erasure. Erasure prevents and has prevented Black experts from moving closer to the center of where power operates in organizations or in institutions. Sometimes it's about being structurally excluded from the rooms, and sometimes it's the terms of our inclusion in the room. You're allowed in the building but not on the tenth floor, or once you get there, you can't access the glass offices in the back.

Over the last five to seven years, largely due to Black Lives Matter and subsequent white reactionary politics, the boundaries of rational debate have either expanded or exploded or both. So if you are a space, a platform, an institution that is part of the infrastructure of the public discourse, and you are not at this point affirmatively putting forward Black expertise as one of the valences of your institution or organization, you are de facto a part of the white counterresponse to Blackness.

The Black Agenda has come at a moment when people are reimagining what the boundaries are between academic and public discourse. And this is the moment when we need most the voices who understand the discourse and also understand what the stakes are in Black lives—that is, Black scholars.

The Black Agenda also puts forward a model for what's considered good public intellectualism while showcasing that there is no shortage of people who do that work. This book takes away the excuse of "Well, we just don't know where to look" or this idea that "I didn't come through these communities, so you can't fault me for not knowing" while lowering the opportunity cost of learning about different types of expertise and drawing on them. The book moves past the dispassionate and unpolarized space that many seem to strive for and instead asserts the following: if you are not centering Black expertise, you are becoming a vacuum for white rage.

The Black Agenda asks and answers important questions so that we can align our economic behaviors with our social and cultural values. I think of this book as doing a version of that for the public discourse: Which institutions deserve credibility and trust at this moment? Are they the ones that use this book to help shape how they build the audience's taste and preferences for who should be an expert? When you take off the table that "we can't know" or "we don't know," then you can reallocate your responsibility for the problem, and people become implicated in a very direct kind of way because they can't use that excuse anymore.

The Black Agenda is the opening salvo of how an institution is valued as well as a guide to people's investments, both at an individual and institutional level. If you are a gatekeeper at an organization, at an institution, or in a community, you should be reading this book as a check on what your natural biases are toward who should belong, who belongs in the room, and who doesn't. And make no mistake, this book applies broadly to gatekeepers across any institution, from your community nonprofit to the local newspaper to MSNBC and beyond. If you gatekeep any critical resource, and that can be from money to attention, you should be reading this book.

At the end of the day, *The Black Agenda* is a litmus test, but more importantly, this book is the first step toward defining Black expertise, assigning value to the work that we do, and taking up space in the public on our own terms.

I, for one, am looking forward to being able to knock people on the head with the collection. I'm looking forward to the spaces in need of critical self-reflection that make this book a normal part of routine business and the discourse. And most of all, I am looking forward to everybody with any resource, no matter how small, reading this book too.

EDITOR'S INTRODUCTION

Growing up, I was sometimes too ashamed to raise my hand and admit that I didn't understand something. Doing so, I feared, would put my ignorance on full display, thus affirming those who already presumed my lack of knowledge given that I am Black and a woman. What I found as I got older, however, was that in daring to reveal what I did not know, I liberated those around me who were just as confused as I was.

When March 2020 rolled around, I was well practiced at asking questions, and I wasn't the only one looking for answers. From reporters to teachers to parents to Twitter, everyone was desperately searching for a way out of a global pandemic that had managed to successfully disrupt and ravage the lives of people across the world.

Amid the confusion and chaos, what I most wanted to understand, as an emerging researcher, was why public discourse about a global pandemic, which disproportionately impacted Black communities, was largely absent of Black perspectives. I wanted to know why people who looked like me were being silenced by media outlets that claimed to cover the whole truth, when the biggest stories at the time seemed to be about the compounding crises of COVID-19, massive unemployment, and economic insecurity for Black families across the country. So, I decided to raise my hand and ask a question: Do Black experts matter?

While the answer is obvious—yes, of course Black experts matter—nearly everyone in the mainstream, prior to the racial justice protests in the summer of 2020, would have you believe otherwise. The glaring omission of Black experts is so commonplace across Western society that it has become normalized.

It is not normal, however, to ignore, silence, and misrepresent a substantial share of the country or pick one or two people to represent millions amid life-altering crises. It is not normal to minimize what is happening to Black people in America, especially those who are descendants of the enslaved people who built this country. And in the summer of 2020, after four hundred years and some change, in the wake of nationwide and global protests surrounding the murders of George Floyd and Breonna Taylor, non-Black people and institutions across the country publicly acknowledged this abnormality for a brief period of time.

The summer had seemingly become an inflection point. Suddenly, every public-facing entity, from celebrities to organizations to publicly traded companies, seemed to recognize that refusing to denounce anti-Black racism had damaging consequences. Yet as public discourse shifted around racial justice in health care, climate, and the like, I was only left with more questions: Why were Black experts and researchers *still* being ignored at this critical moment in our country and the world's history? Why were the same people posting "#BlackLivesMatter," refusing to legitimize what Black experts knew and had known this entire time? If Black experts did indeed matter, why was no one listening to them?

Unfortunately, the momentum of summer 2020 seemed to be short-lived. While Black experts were being tapped to join initiatives aimed at "racial healing" and "diversity, equity, and inclusion," efforts in support of Black Lives Matter were reduced to occasional articles centering Black stories and Black boxes on Instagram (yes, people did this and thought that it was sufficient).

Dismayingly, Professor Hakeem Jefferson of Stanford and Professor Jennifer Chudy of Wellesley College found that in months leading up to the summer of 2021, there was even *less* support for Black Lives Matter than there was prior to the start of 2020. In other words, whatever gains were made in the summer of 2020 disappeared once the mainstream hype died down. Acknowledging systemic racism cannot be hype-driven. There is no silver-bullet solution to a four-centuries-long (and counting!) problem. What is needed now are solutions, daring ones, that will ensure that the current and next generation is better off.

May I submit to you that if anti-Black racism colors a myriad of issues from the economy to student loan debt to climate change, then Black experts should be driving the narrative instead of waiting to be called in? Black experts matter now more than ever because they are not just critical to providing us with the tools and language to decipher a world bent on undermining Black life—they are also equipped to provide the backdrop of lived experience that further contextualizes their expertise. Experience is the difference between studying racial inequality and living through it.

My questions about how Black expertise can shape the future inspired the collection you are about to read. While this book began as an ode to Black economists and policy wonks, the intersectional nature of our country's most pressing issues necessarily broadened the project's scope to encompass an array of subjects that now includes, but is not limited to, perspectives from nurses, educators, epidemiologists, AI researchers, lawyers, and climate advocates.

The collection shines a light on Black experts from all over who draw on their extensive expertise to suggest ways forward toward a country, and world, where the humanity of Black people, especially Black Americans, is fully realized.

WHAT *THE BLACK AGENDA* IS NOT:

The Black Agenda **is not exhaustive.** It does not touch every issue. It is an *attempt* to bridge the gap between learning about anti-racist philosophies and crafting solutions that center and celebrate Black people. It does not include the full spectrum of important contributions from thought leaders, writers, and activists who do the work that helps shape the fullest picture of racial justice in our country.

The Black Agenda **is not a bandage.** Reading this book or even implementing the solutions in this book will neither solve racism nor excuse the bigotry that lines the pockets of the most powerful. Should individuals and institutions read, reflect, and adopt these ideas? Of course. Is this book justifying the avoidance of other bold and transformative ideas beyond the collection? Absolutely not. This book is not a short-lived read to pacify guilt. This is about a way forward, one that includes us all.

WHAT *THE BLACK AGENDA* IS:

The Black Agenda **is a love letter to Black experts,** one that acknowledges the tireless and relentless work of Black research and policy experts that often goes unnoticed. These essays also depict how Black scholarship can and should inform public discourse that inevitably and disproportionately impacts Black life.

***The Black Agenda* is one place to start.** The issues outlined throughout the collection may be familiar to those who have lived through them, but the collection also offers specific solutions to begin tackling the lived and painful experience of Black people in the U.S. It is an ode to hope. Not every essay will resonate with each reader, and that is to be expected.

In the collection, I do not take a specific position on any of the issues discussed. Rather, I serve as your student-guide, learning alongside you. Each chapter features several essays that ultimately point to solutions that aim to transform our country while proposing ways to uproot systemic racism. And yes, it is intentional that many of the contributing authors are Black women. I believe unequivocally that listening to and centering Black women is America's first step toward justice fully realized. *The Black Agenda: Bold Solutions for a Broken System* is a preview into an America that honors Black identity in some of the most important facets of society for years to come. In the words of James Baldwin, "Not everything that is faced can be changed, but nothing can be changed until it is faced."

PART I
CLIMATE

Climate change is not the Great Equalizer. It is the Great Multiplier.

—MARY ANNAÏSE HEGLAR

Over the course of the past two decades, there has been increasing attention paid to the climate crisis by way of young activists and movements, such as the March for Science. What is unequivocally clear based on the evidence is that the earth is indeed in crisis. This crisis will, and already has had, lasting and devastating effects, particularly for Black and Brown communities globally despite largely being seen as a concern for well-off white individuals and communities.

The Black [CLIMATE] Agenda shows that the narrative around climate change cannot be limited to melting ice caps and paper straws. The authors emphasize the need for systemic actions in place of performative acts. Ultimately, this chapter introduces readers to the environmental reality faced by Black people who live at the intersection of multiple crises through the lens of climate scientists, communicators, and advocates. In the chapter, expect to hear from:

- The former president of the American Meteorological Society, **Marshall Shepherd,** who writes about the weather-climate gap that makes the new wave of climate-induced storms an even bigger threat for Black communities living in environmentally vulnerable areas. He argues that the climate crisis is fundamentally a civil rights issue and warrants building equitable policies.

- A member of the Intersectional Environmentalist Council, **Abigail Abhaer Adekunbi Thomas,** who makes a case for why the term *intersectional environmentalism* must become more than a buzzword and translate into action that challenges the very foundations of systems that oppress marginalized communities. Her solutions touch on abolition, criminal justice, and more.

- Climate communicator, writer, and cohost of the podcast *Hot Take,* **Mary Annaïse Heglar,** who has spent the better part of a decade noting how the climate justice movement has unfolded. Her essay emphasizes the importance of centering the climate justice movement squarely on Black lives by asking the climate space to stop #AllLivesMattering the climate crisis.

- And finally, **arii lynton-smith,** a nonbinary creative, discusses how newfound mainstream interest in sustainability is not so new for Queer Black creatives, who have opted for sustainable lifestyles throughout the entirety of their lives. They go on to emphasize how Queer theory in particular can be used as one way to begin thinking about how Black people interact with the space of environmentalism and sustainability, and why that matters.

THE WEATHER-CLIMATE GAP AND THE BLACK COMMUNITY

Marshall Shepherd

Climate change undoubtedly represents one of the most formidable challenges of our time. Yet some of the most vulnerable populations would likely challenge me on that statement. When faced with "kitchen table" issues like health care, monthly grocery bills, or heating the home, many people from marginalized communities are tempted to view climate change as a theoretical, academic construct about a starving polar bear, or only relevant to the distant future. In reality, the climate crisis is very much about those same familiar issues that Black America grapples with daily.

Studies continue to show that African American communities are disproportionately affected by climate-related hazards, such as heat, drought, hurricanes, and flooding, while accounting for a relatively small percentage of total carbon emissions. This so-called weather-climate gap is rooted in well-understood disparities associated with income, opportunity, and discriminatory practices. This gap presents a unique danger to Black Americans, making a sharper climate focus essential to the Black community's well-being.

As an atmospheric scientist, it has been clear to me for decades that climate change is creating multifaceted risks for society. Our scientific trend lines, models, and analyses have long pointed to a "new normal" featuring intense hurricanes, prolonged heat waves, urban flooding, and debilitating drought. Cornell scholar Dr. Maria Cristina Garcia argues that people have been displaced by climate for thousands of years but that coping with the current crisis will require political will and adaptability of unprecedented scales. In 2005, the aftermath of Hurricane Katrina gave us a glimpse of what the weather-climate gap looks like for certain communities. To deconstruct that glimpse, it is important to explore the concept of vulnerability.

At its core, environmental vulnerability can be framed in terms of exposure and sensitivity. In the case of Katrina, for example, people throughout the Louisiana, Mississippi, and Alabama coastal region were "exposed" to the storm. However, there were also varying degrees of "sensitivity" (injury, harm, economic hardship, or death) to the floods, wind, power outages, and damaged homes among residents of this area. The convergence of these terms represents a measure of weather-climate vulnerability. While the entire region struggled, the faces etched in our minds of those needing shelter, food, and medical care at the Superdome were people of color and the poorest residents of New Orleans. Similar disparities in vulnerability have played out with Hurricane Harvey (2017) and the Chicago Heat Wave (1995). Even in the Caribbean region, people of color were disproportionately displaced by Hurricane Maria (2018).

Climate vulnerability as a function of race is structurally rooted in "place." According to the U.S. Environmental Protection Agency (EPA), Black Americans are more likely to live in urban heat islands, portions of a city that tend to be significantly warmer than surrounding areas due to the abundance of man-made surfaces like asphalt, as well as a lack of vegetation, poor ventilation, and anthropogenic waste heat, or heat generated by human beings. In 2020, a study published in the *Journal of the American Planning Association* revealed that historical redlining practices might also account for some of these disparities. Redlining early in the twentieth century, the practice of outlining poor and minority neighborhoods with a red outline for bankers, lenders, and insurers, led to underlying climate injustices. The environmental justice movement grew out of recognition that industry viewed Black communities as dumping grounds for waste and locations for undesirable industries.

The "climate justice" movement must address the weather-climate gap. As Professor Robert Bullard, the Father of Environmental Justice, has articulated with fervor, zip code or "living on the wrong side of the tracks" should not determine one's risk or vulnerability to an extreme weather event. Yet the evidence clearly establishes that it does. A study emerging from my research group at the University of Georgia by Neil Debbage, now at the University of Texas–San Antonio, found that African Americans in the Atlanta-to-Charlotte urban corridor were more likely to live in flood-prone areas.

The inequities of climate change are further amplified by the fact that the largest percentage of Black people resides in Southern states or cities. These regions experience the full suite of climatic hazards, including heat, hurricanes, tornadoes, drought, flooding, snowstorms, and wildfires. Communities will continue to struggle as such events increase in intensity or frequency. As a whole, African Americans lag behind in income, have higher health disparities, and have inadequate insurance. Heat waves, landfalling hurricanes, and flooding further amplify an already unequal burden. So what do we do?

African American communities must become more "climate-centric." It is important to view climate change as an economic, health, and societal threat in the same way that we view COVID-19 or a recession. Communities must take ownership of climate planning and adaptation strategies that address the social disparities outlined. Disaster management planning and mitigation strategies must be developed and implemented in anticipation of future threats rather than as a reaction to an episodic event. From a political perspective, African Americans must vote with the climate crisis in mind on the local, state, and national levels. Ultimately, however, the weather-climate gap will not disappear until racial wealth inequality disappears.

The "new energy" economy of solar, wind, and other sources creates an unprecedented opportunity for mitigating this inequality. The African American community must be positioned to benefit from and leverage this new economic reality. Put another way, we must be trained in blue-collar and STEM-based jobs, prepare our communities for new infrastructure, and envision new economic realities in a non-fossil-fuels-based economy. It remains to be seen whether a "Green New Deal" will garner enough bipartisan support to flourish, but there will likely be some action along such lines in the future. Are we ready?

Dr. Martin Luther King's *Letter from Birmingham Jail* was written with a charge for community action and a stance against racial injustice. However, his poignant remarks are relevant herein.

I am cognizant of the interrelatedness of all communities and states. I cannot sit idly by in Atlanta and not be concerned about Birmingham. Injustice anywhere is a threat to justice everywhere. We are caught in an inescapable network of mutuality, tied in a single garment of destiny. Whatever affects one directly, affects all indirectly.

Before joining the faculty at the University of Georgia, I spent twelve years of my career as a scientist at NASA's Goddard Space Flight Center. We studied Earth as a system because the atmosphere, oceans, cryosphere, and biosphere are all interconnected. Just as Dr. King saw a network of mutuality in the Civil Rights Movement, I see it in our shared vulnerability and response to climate change. The weather-climate gap is fundamentally an issue of civil rights, and we must approach it as such to create a safe and equitable world for all.

Works Cited

Debbage, Neil. "Multiscalar Spatial Analysis of Urban Flood Risk and Environmental Justice in the Charlanta Megaregion, USA." *Anthropocene* 28 (2019): 100226. https://www.sciencedirect.com/science/article/abs/pii/S2213305419300372.

EPA. "Heat Islands and Equity." http://epa.gov/heatislands/heat-islands-and-equity.

Wilson, Bev. "Urban Heat Management and the Legacy of Redlining." *Journal of the American Planning Association* 86, no. 4 (2020): 443–457. doi: 10.1080/01944363.2020.1759127. https://www.tandfonline.com/doi/full/10.1080/01944363.2020.1759127.

INTERSECTIONAL ENVIRONMENTALISM MUST SHAPE CLIMATE ACTION

Abigail Abhaer Adekunbi Thomas

ntersectionality, a term coined by civil rights advocate and critical race theory scholar Kimberlé Crenshaw, has sparked critical conversations and discourse for many years on how gender, race, and class interact and impact the way people with multiple marginalized identities experience the world. Crenshaw first introduced the world to intersectionality in 1989 with her paper "Demarginalizing the Intersection of Race and Sex: A Black Feminist Critique of Antidiscrimination Doctrine, Feminist Theory and Antiracist Politics," which explores how Black American women's oppression is compounded by race, class, and gender discrimination. In her analysis, Crenshaw illustrates how an intersectional framework acknowledges and centers the multiple oppressed identities of Black American women and creates a more holistic and effective approach to addressing racism and sexism.

Although the term *intersectionality* was born out of addressing the nexus of race, gender, and class, it can also be applied more broadly to address global issues like the climate crisis. The framework of intersectional environmentalism incorporates Crenshaw's theory and applies it to challenge one-dimensional solutions to environmental and climate issues. Many environmentalists and organizations, including Robert Bullard, known as the Father of Environmental Justice; Generation Green, which coined the term and theory of environmental liberation; and more recently the Intersectional Environmentalist, the organization who developed and shaped the term *intersectional environmentalism* in 2020, have incorporated and expanded Crenshaw's theory into conversations around climate action. They continue to prove that intersectional environmentalism is the only path forward toward creating transformative and lasting solutions toward addressing climate change.

Intersectional environmentalism provides the holistic perspective that advocating for environmental protection includes dismantling the oppressive social, economic, and political systems that perpetuate harm, especially for marginalized communities who are disproportionately impacted by climate change. It recognizes that without addressing the systemic issues that are impacting our world today, we cannot successfully make environmental progress that benefits everyone, not just the handful of those who are privileged and will not bear disproportionate effects of climate change. Furthermore, by incorporating an intersectional lens to environmentalism, we can see how environmental issues directly relate to and are a product of capitalism, white supremacy, and colonialism. While at first the concept of intersectional environmentalism may seem overwhelming or too expansive to practically incorporate into climate action moving forward, it actually supports a targeted method of understanding and addressing climate action in a way that dismantles multiple issues altogether.

We consistently see the success of an intersectional frame of mind through environmental justice wins from the termination of the Keystone XL oil pipeline in the U.S. and Canada to the court ruling in Mombasa, Kenya, where Owino Uhuru settlement residents were compensated for the health effects their community endured from a local battery recycling facility in the area. In both instances, acknowledging the degradation of the planet and the devastating impacts these issues place on communities was critical in challenging the status quo of short-term economic interests from large corporations. Not only did these victories combat major environmental issues, but they also addressed critical public health and human rights issues. Having seen success in incorporating intersectional environmentalism into localized environmental and climate movements, the next logical step is to apply these tactics and climate actions to address the root causes and the outcomes of climate change.

One of the best ways to do this is through more collaboration and solidarity between climate and abolitionist movements. Prison abolition, abolition democracy, and environmental justice are all linked and directly rooted in the same systems of white supremacy, heteropatriarchy, and capitalism that perpetuate harm across various communities. This interconnectedness is a tremendous hazard, but also our biggest strength. This strength comes not only from solidarity across movements but in the resources, tools, experiences, and knowledge that can be shared between communities. Through unification, we can create spaces that cultivate collective action and movement building that can drive major structural, inclusive changes.

While most people think of prison abolition as purely a social justice issue, prison systems are also a major environmental injustice. Both social and political prisoners globally are among the most vulnerable to the effects of climate change and are also directly impacted by environmental pollution. Most prisons do not meet environmental and public health regulations, and are usually near landfills, mines, and toxic waste dumps, especially in the U.S., where roughly 589 or more federal and state prisons are within three miles of Superfund cleanup sites, which are known to be hazardous commercial waste sites that require long-term and extensive cleanup programs. This exemplifies a major environmental injustice in areas such as the U.S. and UK, because a majority of prisoners are low-income Black, Indigenous, or people of color, which makes them disproportionately impacted by environmental pollution and hazards. In fact, according to the Abolitionist Law Center and the Human Rights Coalition in their 2014 yearlong review *No Escape,* 80 percent of inmates at SCI Fayette in Pennsylvania were reported to suffer from respiratory, throat, and sinus infections due to their exposure to coal ash. Furthermore, capitalism plays a large role in exacerbating environmental and public health issues in prisons due to the prison industrial complex. The prison industrial complex describes how governments, private prison industry, companies, and law enforcement work together to fuel, exploit, and profit off the criminal justice system and imprisonment of people. In addition to these realities, the prison-industrial complex has a substantial impact on industrial emissions. According to a Portland State University study, mass incarceration and the increased rate of imprisonment have links to emissions in the U.S. due to the billion-dollar industry of private prisons. The construction of new prisons, the resources associated with building these new prisons, and the renovations and expansion of existing prisons all make significant contributions to fossil fuel emissions. Companies also use cheap prison labor to increase profits, driving up production and thus pollution, capitalism, and the serious environmental health impacts incarcerated people face every day without adequate health care.

Just as these injustices compound one another, sharing solutions and ideas across movements can be instrumental in combating oppression. Restorative justice, a practice rooted in Indigenous cultures throughout the world, is a concept used in the prison abolition framework in the U.S. It encourages solutions to repair the harm caused by crime offenders against victims. This has been presented as an alternative to incarceration, which could restore all parties involved when a crime has occurred. Studies have shown that it effectively reduces repeat offenses as well as reduces post-traumatic stress symptoms for victims and provides more tangible and long-term satisfaction and justice for victims. If we also use restorative justice solutions to climate issues, we can come up with stronger forms of accountability, like *climate reparations,* a term coined by Maxine Burkett, for environmental crimes and injustices. Using reparations as a tool to address and acknowledge the harm created by climate to the Majority World could also be an extremely effective tool to use as a step toward transformative climate justice for communities who have been negatively impacted by climate change, environmental pollution, and health issues.

In addition to prison abolition, there is a significant space for the climate movement to step into and work alongside the abolition democracy movement. Abolition democracy is a framework developed by American civil rights leader W. E. B. Du Bois in his book *Black Reconstruction in America,* where he examines how systems of oppression are foundational and deeply embedded in the U.S. government. The U.S. continues to illustrate this fragmented system through the current wave of voter suppression laws that predominantly impact voters of color, low-income communities, LGBTQ+ voters, and voters with disabilities, who face increasing environmental injustice. The disenfranchisement of marginalized groups impacts communities' ability to make radical political and cultural shifts and vote for their health, safety, and future. Centuries of diluting votes and inhibiting communities from voting against harmful policies and politicians has continued the cycle of environmental and social degradation to keep harmful systems and people in power. This is why it is critical for the voting rights movement and the environmental movement to work together on voting structures that build people power and support spaces for voters to see the impacts their votes have on their community.

Both restorative justice and abolition democracy can and should pave the way for additional resources to be redirected toward global systemic issues like colonialism, which has also exacerbated the impacts of climate change for the Majority World or middle- to lower-income countries. Among the many pieces of abolition democracy is the U.S. government's reliance on imperialism and neocolonialism in the Majority World. Not only does this form of oppression perpetuate extraction, but it also exacerbates climate and environmental injustice. Most U.S.-based multinational corporations have their operations in Majority World countries, where environmental and social regulations are less stringent than regulations in the U.S. or any other country in the West. This concentration of production, coupled with the deregulation and monitoring of production, exposes vulnerable communities living near or working in these production sites to environmental pollution and health impacts.

The links between prison abolition, abolition democracy, and environmental justice illustrate how combining and integrating these efforts would promote extremely effective and powerful solutions to environmental, social, and political issues globally. Incorporating abolition into the intersectional environmental framework provides climate action with more of a solution-oriented viewpoint that focuses on how we can rethink the cultural, political, and economic systems that exacerbate and fuel climate change. It should be central to all climate action whether policy, on-the-ground efforts, or in environmental education. When we begin to look at environmentalism through a holistic perspective that embraces innovative, regenerative, and transformative solutions, we address some of the larger institutions and structures that environmental issues are built upon and understand that the best path forward for both the planet and people is to provide solutions that liberate marginalized communities and abolish all systems of oppression.

Works Cited

Bernd, Candice, et al. "America's Toxic Prisons: The Environmental Injustices of Mass Incarceration." *Earth Island Journal.* https://earthisland.org/journal/americas-toxic-prisons/.

Burkett, Maxine. "Climate Reparations." *Melbourne Journal of International Law* 10, 2009. https://ssrn.com/abstract=1539726.

"Climate Change Is an Increasing Threat to Africa." UN Climate Change, October 27, 2020. https://unfccc.int/news/climate-change-is-an-increasing-threat-to-africa.

"Court Ruling Called a Milestone in Environmental Justice." United Nations Human Rights Office of the High Commissioner, September 7, 2020. https://www.ohchr.org/EN/NewsEvents/Pages/LeadPollutionJudgement.aspx.

Crenshaw, Kimberlé. "Demarginalizing the Intersection of Race and Sex: A Black Feminist Critique of Antidiscrimination Doctrine, Feminist Theory and Antiracist Politics." *University of Chicago Legal Forum,* vol. 1989, issue 1, article 8. https://chicagounbound.uchicago.edu/uclf/vol1989/iss1/8.

Emissions Gap Report 2020. Nairobi: United Nations Environment Programme, 2020.

Greene, Robert, II. "The Legacy of Black Reconstruction." *Jacobin,* August 27, 2018. https://www.jacobinmag.com/2018/08/web-du-bois-black-reconstruction-civil-rights.

Greenfield, Nicole. "The Connection Between Mass Incarceration and Environmental Justice." NRDC, January 19, 2018. https://www.nrdc.org/onearth/connection-between-mass-incarceration-and-environmental-justice.

Jones, Alexi. "Visualizing the Unequal Treatment of LGBTQ People in the Criminal Justice System." Prison Policy Initiative, March 2, 2021. https://www.prisonpolicy.org/blog/2021/03/02/lgbtq/.

"Kimberlé Crenshaw on Intersectionality, More Than Two Decades Later." Columbia Law School, June 8, 2017. https://www.law.columbia.edu/news/archive/kimberle-crenshaw-intersectionality-more-two-decades-later.

Lipsitz, George. "Abolition Democracy and Global Justice." *Comparative American Studies* 2, no. 3 (2004): 277–280. doi: 10.1177/1477570004047906.

"Mass Incarceration." American Civil Liberties Union, July 22, 2021. https://www.aclu.org/issues/smart-justice/mass-incarceration.

McDaniel, Dustin S., et al. *No Escape: Exposure to Toxic Coal Waste at State Correctional Institution Fayette.* Philadelphia: Abolitionist Law Center and Human Rights Coalition, 2004.

McGee, Julius Alexander, et al. "Locked into Emissions: How Mass Incarceration Contributes to Climate Change." *Social Currents* (2020): 1–15. https://www.academia.edu/44608809/Locked_into_Emissions_How_Mass_Incarceration_Contributes_to_Climate_Change.

"Prison Reform and Alternatives to Imprisonment." United Nations Office on Drugs and Crime, July 22, 2021. https://www.unodc.org/unodc/en/justice-and-prison-reform/prison-reform-and-alternatives-to-imprisonment.html.

Sherman, L. W., and H. Strang. *Restorative Justice: The Evidence.* London: Smith Institute, 2007.

Smith, Earl, and Angela Hattery. "The Prison Industrial Complex." *Sociation Today* 4, no. 2 (2006): 1. https://www.ncsociology.org/sociationtoday/v42/prison.htm.

United States Department of Justice and Zhen Zeng. *Jail Inmates*

in 2018. Washington, D.C.: Bureau of Justice Statistics, 2020.
https://bjs.ojp.gov/content/pub/pdf/ji18.pdf.

Washington, John. "What Is Prison Abolition?" *Nation,* August 1,
2018. https://www.thenation.com/article/archive/what-is-prison
-abolition/.

"What Is a Superfund?" Environmental Protection Agency.
Accessed August 3, 2021. https://www.epa.gov/superfund/what
-superfund.

Yasin, Baber, and Georgina Sturge. "Ethnicity and the Criminal
Justice System: What Does Recent Data Say on Over-
Representation?" UK Parliament, October 2, 2020. https://
commonslibrary.parliament.uk/ethnicity-and-the-criminal
-justice-system-what-does-recent-data-say/.

STOP #ALLLIVESMATTERING
THE CLIMATE CRISIS
Mary Annaïse Heglar

The summer of 2020 was unlike anything I'd ever seen. The streets filled with shouts of "Black Lives Matter!" and clamors for justice that carried through the day and into the night and then into the next day. Americans ventured out of the social isolation imposed by the COVID-19 pandemic and into the streets in all fifty states, inspiring protests around the world.

Many sources would say that it started with the killing of George Floyd by a Minneapolis police officer in late May. Or with the racial profiling of a Black birder by the name of Christian Cooper in New York's Central Park that occurred on the same day as Floyd's death. Still more might take it back to the police murder of Breonna Taylor or the vigilante murder of Ahmaud Arbery earlier in the year. But Black folks knew that this outrage had been simmering for months, years, generations. This tinderbox has been burning since the first kidnapping *four hundred years ago.*

To be clear, police murders are, sadly, nothing new. In fact, the murder of George Floyd was eerily reminiscent of the 2014 murder of Eric Garner in New York. But whereas Garner's murder drew condemnations of Staten Island and Trayvon

Martin's elicited the same sentiment for Florida, in the summer of 2020, no such distinctions were made. It was as though state lines and city borders had been swept away as we all sat isolated in our homes. This was different. This was big.

Even in the climate movement—which has long stuck to the sidelines in moments like this—advocates and organizations have publicly declared that Black Lives Matter. They have finally stood up and spoken out in defense of Black people's right to breathe. And it's about damn time.

There is just one problem: this new commitment to Black people has often come with the assumption that the fight for climate justice had to pause. As a "Climate Person," my social media feeds were awash with calls to pause climate activism for the sake of supporting Black people, as though the two were mutually exclusive. As a Black Climate Person, I can't tell you how disorienting that was.

Up until a few years ago, there used to be a myth in environmental circles that Black people don't care about the environment or about climate issues. There's a lot of data to prove that that's not true. But I don't need that data, because I've been around Black people my whole life, and I've never met one who didn't care about the environment or about animals. I've met plenty, though, who don't care for environmentalists. And I understand why.

Typically, when the environmental movement has attempted to reach out to Black communities, it turns into something I've called *existential exceptionalism*. The conversation goes something like this: "Oh, you're worried about police violence? Well, you need to be worried about these POLAR BEARS!" Climate change is framed as the issue that threatens "all of us" and therefore should be everyone's priority. Climate change, the myth goes, is the Great Equalizer. Not only is this approach dismissive and insensitive, the premise is simply untrue.

It's been documented again and again that climate change hurts Black people first and worst—both in the United States and globally. Moreover, Black people have done the *least* to create the problem, and our systemic oppression runs directly parallel to the climate crisis.

Climate change takes any problem you already had, any threat you were already under, and multiplies it. When you take a population that has lived in chronic crisis, under constant threat, for generations—from police violence to housing discrimination to general disenfranchisement—and add yet another threat? That's not just a recipe for catastrophe, it's a recipe for collapse. With the climate crisis itself—the storms and the temperatures—it's not so much that the game is rigged, it's the playing field. Climate change is not the Great Equalizer. It is the Great Multiplier.

So it's not just time to talk about climate—it's time to talk about it as the Black issue it is. It's time to stop whitewashing it. In other words, it's time to stop #AllLivesMattering the climate crisis.

It's time to talk about how extreme heat begets extreme violence—and how that can interact with an already extremely violent police force. It's time to talk about what happens in prisons, which often lack air conditioning and heat, as temperatures skyrocket. It's time to talk about climate gentrification and all the people pushed out of their homes in places like Miami and Houston and New Orleans. It's time to talk about the use of tear gas—which hurts respiratory systems during a pandemic that already disproportionately affects Black people—as environmental racism.

And, while we're at it, it's time to talk about why Black people face higher rates of COVID-19 infection and death: because we're far more likely to live in food deserts, and near dumping grounds, power plants, and large-scale animal farms, all of which saddle us with preexisting conditions like asthma, diabetes, and heart disease. Those are the same preexisting conditions that authorities initially attempted to blame for the deaths of Eric Garner and George Floyd.

It's time to talk about what Hurricane Katrina revealed, and what I can never, ever unsee: When disaster strikes, the power structure will either abandon us or turn even more sharply against us. When resources run low, we will have the least, and when we try to take what we need, we'll be labeled looters and shot on sight.

It's time to talk about the white vigilantes who roamed New Orleans after Katrina—and were damn-near state-sanctioned—and today's armed militia groups that are ready and willing to exploit any disaster (including the current protests) to bring about a race war. In fact, in late summer 2020, these same militias took advantage of the wildfires on the West Coast, set up blockades, and harassed people of color who tried to get out of harm's way.

It's time to talk about my biggest fear about the climate crisis. It's not "How will we treat each other?" It's "How will white people treat people who look like me?"

If caring about climate change and caring about Black people were mutually exclusive, I never would have gotten into climate justice. Black people are my first and true love. I don't know who anyone else thought I was fighting for. I got into climate justice work *because* I love Black people. The climate movement needs to decide whether or not it does too.

CENTERING BLACK QUEER
CREATIVES IN SUSTAINABILITY

arii lynton-smith

I find sustainability to be a touchy subject for many of my Black Queer peers. Though it feels like I'm surrounded by folks who are recycling and conscious about reusing and reducing, my peers are quick to make it known that they are *not* environmentalist in any way. I've come to understand this phenomenon as a result of the fact that fads or trends that white influencers are profiting from are practices that many Black people grew up with.

In my house, we didn't throw away containers that we bought from the store if they could be reused for other purposes. We never left the lights on, because a cheaper bill meant more money for other things. We never wasted food, and we always prioritized imaginative ways to use up what we had before it went bad. We shopped at the thrift store and repaired our clothes. We were doing zero-waste swaps before they were viral internet hacks, not because it was *aesthetic* but because it was survival. When I found out my passion for reducing and reusing was characterized as environmentalism, I was not only shocked by the existence of this discipline, but also by the lack of so-called leaders who looked like me.

Not only has it been a struggle to find Black sustainability creatives or content creators across platforms like Instagram,

YouTube, and blogs but also finding folks who are Black and Queer creatives in sustainability has felt nearly impossible. (Creatives may also be considered influencers, but not all influencers are creatives. The key difference is that creatives make content that is informative around a specific topic.) There is a common misconception that there are no Black Queer sustainability influencers and creatives because Black people don't care about the planet. The truth is that white influencers are often exalted for doing the bare minimum and rarely credit the Black creatives they get ideas from. Their oversaturation of the sustainability and environmental justice space has made it nearly impossible for me to find Black voices like Addie Fisher, Tiffany Alexander, Christine Platt, Wawa Gatheru, and Black Queer creator Jupiter. Upon recognizing this absence, I decided to take up space by creating for those existing at the intersection of Queer theory, Black liberation, and Sustainability.

Queer theory aims to "subvert and deconstruct processes of heteronormativity and traditional models of gender and sexuality." It's all about challenging the ideology that promotes heterosexuality as "normal," labeling anything else as *other*. Black liberation theory is similar. The latter talks about deconstructing white supremacy and eradicating the harm it perpetuates to us through anti-Blackness. Both Queer theory and Black liberation, at their core, exist to envision a world that treats Black Queer people better, and for the environmentalism movement to flourish, the space needs to be just that.

Acknowledging the needs of Black Queer creatives is one place for institutions and white creatives to start. In my experience, it is far more likely that Black Queer creatives on my Instagram feed will be asking for rent support or help with groceries. Imagine trying to create when you also have to worry about not getting evicted or being fed. By recognizing the disparity of resources, an easy first step for white creatives is to challenge their collectives and peers to compensate Black creatives for their labor. *Nobody* wants to work for free, and Black Queer folks often *can't* make the sacrifice. Moreover, drawing on Queer theory to make environmentalism and sustainability equitable boils down to achieving a lifestyle where we *all* can freely exist outside the restrictions capitalism places on us. In her book *Braiding Sweetgrass,* Robin Wall Kimmerer writes about the ways in which humanity needs the planet just as much as the planet needs humanity, which is why white creatives and predominantly white institutions must go above and beyond to support those who identify with marginalized communities such as being Black and Queer.

With that in mind, it is impossible to learn from Black Queer creatives if you refuse to listen to us. If you aren't hearing Black Queer perspectives, take a moment to consider if that's because you've started the meeting before we've entered the room. Part of Queer and liberation theory is learning to redefine the ways in which we understand working and productivity. Heteropatriarchy, which prioritizes dollars over humans, will tell you that if someone isn't responding within a two-day window, they are uninterested; or that if a person is ten minutes late to work, then they deserve to be fired. These kinds of conditioning often lead folks to ignore the ideas of Black Queer creatives with no regard to the aforementioned difficulties that they more often have than their white straight counterparts. Patience is key when working with Black Queer creatives. We don't operate on the same timeline as the heteropatriarchy, and we understand that good creativity takes time. Most importantly, we understand that no amount of money is worth sacrificing our well-being.

At the end of the day, if you want to center Black Queer creatives in environmental and sustainability spaces, then actually center us—send us your brand deals, include us in your projects. Instead of trying to learn more about a particular topic that you don't specialize in, pass that job along to a Black Queer peer who does have the knowledge and expertise. Not only do we benefit from the exposure and the money, but you have also shown the brand and/or organization that your network is also an asset they can use. You show them that you prioritize the quality of the work you provide and the quality of work that they receive. Wealth hoarding (or project hoarding) doesn't create a pathway toward liberation.

For my fellow white influencers and creatives, I challenge you all to dig deeper into the ways you can support creatives like me. We won't improve our world by buying every bamboo toothbrush and barefoot shoe on the market. Mason jars will not free us, and the amount of trash you have in your home will not provide opportunities for yourself or others. Centering Queer people, especially Black Queer people, is about learning to move in a way that puts balance back in the equation. Learning to center us liberates us all.

Works Cited

Kidd, Kenneth B., and Derritt Mason, eds. *Queer as Camp: Essays on Summer, Style, and Sexuality.* New York: Fordham University Press, 2019.

Kimmerer, Robin Wall. *Braiding Sweetgrass.* Minneapolis, MN: Milkweed Editions, 2015.

PART II
HEALTH CARE

The structural determinants of health such as the pro-cesses, systems, and policies that lead to inequities in the distribution of resources are central in shaping inequities in housing, employment, and other social determinants of health.

—DARA D. MENDEZ AND JEWEL SCOTT

At the beginning of 2020, few could have expected the world to stop at the hands of a viral infection. COVID-19 laid bare how systemic and institutional racism, globally, impacts the care Black patients receive and the makeup of those providing the care. What became more apparent over the course of 2020 was how the United States has *always* dismissed the health and well-being concerns of Black people. In the midst of the devastation of COVID-19, the crisis also provided an opportunity, however, for Black health care professionals across the nation to voice how the lack of equity in health care undermines how well care is carried out.

The Black [HEALTH CARE] Agenda invites nurses, epidemiologists, and bioethicists—groups often not cited by popular media—to weigh in on what needs to be done to move the U.S. health care system forward. They discuss the need for efforts beyond diversity, equity, and inclusion, push for theoretical frameworks that contextualize the current state of the health care system, and demonstrate the need to legitimize unpaid care work. In the chapter, expect to hear from:

- Epidemiologist **Dara D. Mendez** and nursing researcher **Jewel Scott**, who challenge us to reimagine public health by drawing on theoretical frameworks. They cite public health critical race praxis as a way to guide us to understand how health systems can be reformed for good by emphasizing the need for health practices steeped in racial awareness.

- Nurse and researcher **Monica L. McLemore** discusses the importance of diversity within the health care workforce by examining the health care system's history of exclusion. In her essay, she draws on past evidence to illustrate how the absence of Black people in the health care system ultimately hurts all patients regardless of background and how historically Black higher education institutions can play a role in transforming this reality.

- Philosopher and bioethicist **Yolonda Wilson** outlines why unpaid care work disproportionately affects Black women and how that impacts the way the United States views care work. Her proposed solution is simple: Legitimize care work and use institutions that already support marginalized students to do so.

REENVISIONING PUBLIC HEALTH FOR BLACK AMERICA

Dara D. Mendez and Jewel Scott

The year 2020 brought a convergence of at least three pandemics: COVID-19, racism, and state-sanctioned police violence. The nation's public health system has been flailing for a while, but the intersecting pandemics have laid bare the gaps and deficiencies in the outdated and underfunded public health infrastructure. Disease prevention efforts have largely focused on individual-level behaviors and access to care, and to a much lesser degree, the focus has shifted to social determinants of health such as housing and employment. However, to achieve health equity, the U.S. will have to move even further upstream to address the structural determinants of health. The underlying causes of inequities in housing, employment, and other social determinants of health are structural, defined as the intersecting social processes, systems, and policies that lead to the unequal distribution of resources.

In the U.S., racism is woven into the very origins of the nation, and its lingering effects are evident in the racial wealth gap and residential segregation. Most of the work to improve the nation's health and ensure all populations have the opportunity to live to their fullest potential has not centered on action to remedy the harms of racism. Until recently, only a handful of states (e.g., California, Wisconsin, New York, and Oregon) had implemented approaches to transform their public health systems by focusing on the influence of structural racism. These states employed the systems outlined by the Government Alliance for Race & Equity and suggest that the first step in transforming our public health systems is to normalize racial equity with an explicit focus on race and racism. In our essay, we lift up frameworks such as public health critical race praxis (PHCRP), based on critical race theory (CRT), as critical for interrogating how racism contributes to the racial inequities in COVID-19 and other long-standing health inequities, as well as the national, state, and local responses to these inequities, and for reimagining public health for Black America.

The first two core tenets of CRT and PHCRP are race consciousness and contemporary mechanisms. In other words, the "explicit acknowledgment of the workings of race and racism" and white supremacy in American society and the fact that racism is an ingrained feature in the U.S. is seen as ordinary or normal. Early reports of COVID inequities did not put this data into context or point to the preexisting condition of racism and structural inequity. Furthermore, racism was ingrained not only in the media messaging but also the federal response to COVID-19, particularly in relation to Black communities. For example, the U.S. surgeon general early in the pandemic appeared to blame communities of color when he made comments about "avoid[ing] tobacco, alcohol and drugs." This drew on harmful narratives about Black and Brown communities that are not central to explaining the real disparities in illness.

A third core element is *centering in the margins,* in which the lived experiences, voices, and perspectives of socially marginalized communities are brought to the forefront and lead the discourse. Centering in the margins allows solutions to be developed and drawn from those closest to the problem or issue. Before race-related data and surveillance of COVID-19 became widely available, many Black and Brown scholars and advocates sounded the alarm about the disproportionate impact of COVID-19 on their communities. These communities were vocal because they knew that persistent racial inequities in health care, affordable housing, lack of healthful food, and employment, intersecting with deficiencies in public health infrastructure, would be exacerbated within the context of a pandemic. One example from our work is the Black Equity Coalition, which was established in Allegheny County, Pennsylvania, by a group of Black leaders and non-Black accomplices to provide an equitable and community-driven response to the pandemic.

A fourth element is related to praxis, which is the iterative process of continued learning, self-reflection, and remaining attentive to equity throughout. A commitment to critical race praxis means that no one has "arrived." Instead, there is a constant review, questioning, and shifts in research, scholarship, or practice as needed. The initial guidelines used to determine risk for COVID-19 focused on international travel, consequently underestimating the risk of many Black patients who were exposed via their employment (e.g., frontline workers). Drawing on a praxis rooted in racial justice and health inequity can, and will, provide a critical lens from scientists, practitioners, and the general public. PHCRP honors that learning and knowledge is not exclusively the domain of academics. Instead, CRT values and esteems knowledge from the community. A commitment to continue learning, evolving, reflecting, and shifting are critical to the pursuit of health equity and will require a baseline understanding of how PHCRP and CRT informs racial health outcomes. And one way to approach said commitment is by requiring health care entities and providers to use the R4P approach: Remove, Repair, Restructure, Remediate, and Provide.

R4P is an equity framework that has been applied in the context of public health planning specifically for interrogating systems of oppression with a focus on implementing change in practice or policy. It was developed as a framework to understand the complex set of "contributing factors to health inequities among African-Americans" and to develop specific action steps for evaluation of current approaches and the creation of more equitable approaches. As we reimagine the United States that will emerge from the COVID-19 pandemic, the country has an opportunity to envision a more equitable and just country for Black Americans.

Remove is the specific acknowledgment and removal of power imbalances related to race, class, gender, and other social statuses. The collision of COVID-19 and the repeated killing of unarmed Black men and women led to over one hundred declarations of racism as a public health crisis by local and state governments. These declarations are an important and unprecedented first step, but in reviewing many of the declarations, they largely lack concrete action steps to follow. Next steps for envisioning a healthier Black America will need to include actions that undo racism. For example, the Black Equity Coalition was initially developed in response to the inequitable approach to COVID-19 in the community.

Repair is to understand the historical context and past insults or traumas in order to mitigate the damage. The prime example of repair would be reparations to African American descendants of slaves. An innovative modeling study estimated the COVID-19 pandemic would have been controlled more easily had a reparations program in the form of monetary payments been in existence. The findings suggest that such a reparations program would have reduced the devastating impact of COVID-19 on the Black community through decreased overcrowding in housing and fewer Black individuals in the high-risk (low-compensation) frontline workforce.

Restructure focuses on the existing structures such as policies and norms that should be eliminated to stop the new production of risk. Examples of structural changes recommended by scholars and advocates include: 1) changes in employment (e.g., living wage, universal basic income), 2) universal access to health care and insurance that is not employment-based, and 3) housing (e.g., moratoriums on rent and mortgages and overhauling the housing and banking relationship). All these areas of restructuring are even more pressing when juxtaposed with a pandemic. Experiencing chronic stress, such as financial stressors of being underemployed, contributes to the risk/susceptibility to viral infections. Layer the consequences of an economic downturn with what is already an extensive wealth gap between Black America and others, and a restructuring is long overdue. In reenvisioning the future of Black America, priorities on reparations, unemployment and underemployment, and restructuring pay systems are paramount.

Remediate focuses on addressing communities' immediate needs to "buffer people from the adverse effects" while structural changes are taking place. In the context of COVID-19, many families lost employment or became unhoused, resulting in an increased need for food via food banks or short-term housing moratorium implemented by cities and states to reduce evictions. While restructure is focused on systems and policies, remediate is the concomitant work of reducing risk at the level of the individual. Remediation should occur concurrently with restructuring and might include employment, job retention, and retraining programs for some employment sectors that may not return or that have diminished. Remediation could also include providing birthing support (e.g., doulas) and other health supports that extend beyond COVID testing and vaccination.

Finally, *Provide* focuses on the implementation of interventions that enable disproportionately affected communities to access resources. It furthermore considers how racism, classism, and other forms of oppression will impact the provision, uptake, and perception of services provided. It includes not placing an undue burden on communities to access resources (e.g., requiring a series of meetings before services are rendered) and being flexible in how services and resources are provided. Envisioning the future for Black Americans post-COVID-19 should include culturally responsive and congruent mental health interventions. The collective grief in the U.S. and overwhelmingly in the Black community following this pandemic cannot be overstated. Layered with chronic stress, structural racism, police brutality, and legalized terror, this is a syndemic for tremendous mental health challenges. Mental health in the Black community has been widely underappreciated by scholars. There is a need for interventions that are tailored to the Black experience, delivered by Black and Brown clinicians, and delivered in settings that do not further inconvenience people by forcing them to come into spaces that are unwelcoming and unprepared to address our needs.

Racial inequities in COVID-19 exist in a historical and social context. This context must be acknowledged and brought to the forefront of any work that claims to address these racial inequities. Applying PHCRP, R4P, and other equity-based frameworks throughout the assessing, planning, implementation, evaluation, and any new planning that occurs due to evaluation is essential. This process reduces the risk of exacerbating these inequities while also working toward permanent, structural changes.

Works Cited

Bell, D. A. "Who's Afraid of Critical Race Theory." *University of Illinois Law Review* 1995, no. 4 (1995): 893.

Black Equity Coalition. https://www.blackequitypgh.org/.

Cohen, S. "Psychosocial Vulnerabilities to Upper Respiratory Infectious Illness: Implications for Susceptibility to Coronavirus Disease 2019 (COVID-19)." *Perspectives on Psychological Science* 16, no. 1 (2021): 161.

Cohen, S., E. Frank, W. J. Doyle, D. P. Skoner, B. S. Rabin, and J. M. Gwaltney Jr. "Types of Stressors That Increase Susceptibility to the Common Cold in Healthy Adults." *Health Psychology* 17, no. 3 (1998): 214.

Daniels, R. J., and M. H. Morial. "The Covid-19 Racial Disparities Could Be Even Worse Than We Think." *Washington Post,* April 23, 2020. https://www.washingtonpost.com/opinions/2020/04/23/covid-19-racial-disparities-could-be-even-worse-than-we-think/.

Darity, W. A., Jr., and A. K. Mullen. *From Here to Equality: Reparations for Black Americans in the Twenty-First Century.* Chapel Hill: University of North Carolina Press, 2020.

Dyer, O. "Covid-19: Black People and Other Minorities Are Hardest Hit in US." *BMJ* 369 (2020): m1483. doi: 10.1136/bmj.m1483.

Ford, C. L. "Commentary: Addressing Inequities in the Era of COVID-19: The Pandemic and the Urgent Need for Critical Race Theory." *Family and Community Health* 43, no. 3 (2020): 184–186. doi:10.1097/fch.0000000000000266.

Ford, C. L., and C. O. Airhihenbuwa. "The Public Health Critical Race Methodology: Praxis for Antiracism Research." *Social Science and Medicine* 71, no. 8 (2010): 1390–1398. doi: 10.1016/j.socscimed.2010.07.030.

Ford, C., B. Amani, K. Norris, K. Skrine Jeffers, and R. Akee. "Open Letter: The Need to Prioritize Equity in Policy Responses to the COVID-19 Pandemic." Center for the Study of Racism, Social Justice & Health, April 7, 2020. https://www.racialhealthequity.org/blog/covid19openletter.

Garg, S., L. Kim, M. Whitaker, A. O'Halloran, C. Cummings, R. Holstein, et al. "Hospitalization Rates and Characteristics of Patients Hospitalized with Laboratory-Confirmed Coronavirus Disease 2019-COVID-NET, 14 States, March 1–30, 2020." *MMWR: Morbidity and Mortality Weekly Report* 69, no. 15 (2020): 458–464. doi: 10.15585/mmwr.mm6915e3.

Goldstein, Amy, and Emily Guskin. "Almost One-Third of Black Americans Know Someone Who Died of COVID-19 Survey Shows." *Washington Post,* June 26, 2020. https://www.washingtonpost.com/health/almost-one-third-of-black-americans-know-someone-who-died-of-covid-19-survey-shows/2020/06/25/3ec1d4b2-b563–11ea-aca5-ebb63d27e1ff_story.html.

Gravlee, C. C. "Systemic Racism, Chronic Health Inequities, and COVID-19: A Syndemic in the Making?" *American Journal of Human Biology* 32, no. 5 (2020): e23482. doi: 10.1002/ajhb.23482.

Hogan, V., D. L. Rowley, S. B. White, and Y. Faustin. "Dimensionality and R4P: A Health Equity Framework for Research Planning and Evaluation in African American Populations." *Maternal Child Health Journal* 22, no. 2 (2018): 147–153. doi: 10.1007/s10995-017-2411-z.

Mendez, D., J. Scott, et al. *A Policy Critique and Analysis of Racism as a Public Health Crisis.* Manuscript in progress, 2021.

Rho, H., H. Brown, and S. Fremstad. "A Basic Demographic Profile of Workers in Frontline Industries." Center for Economic

and Policy Research, April 7, 2020. https://cepr.net/a-basic
-demographic-profile-of-workers-in-frontline-industries/.

Richardson, E. T., M. M. Malik, W. A. Darity, A. K. Mullen, M.
E. Morse, M. Malik, et al. "Reparations for American Descendants of Persons Enslaved in the U.S. and their Potential Impact
on SARS-CoV-2 Transmission." *Social Science & Medicine* 276
(2021): 113741. https://doi.org/10.1016/j.socscimed.2021
.113741.

"Risk for COVID-19 Infection, Hospitalization, and Death by
Race & Ethnicity." Centers for Disease Control, February 18,
2021. https://www.cdc.gov/coronavirus/2019-ncov/covid-data
/investigations-discovery/hospitalization-death-by-race-ethnicity
.html.

Solar, O., and A. Irwin. *A Conceptual Framework for Action on the
Social Determinants of Health*. Geneva, Switzerland: WHO Doc-
ument Production Services, 2010.

Troyer, E. A., J. N. Kohn, and S. Hong. "Are We Facing a Crashing
Wave of Neuropsychiatric Sequelae of COVID-19? Neuropsychiatric Symptoms and Potential Immunologic Mechanisms."
Brain, Behavior, and Immunity 87 (2020): 34–39. doi:10.1016/j.
bbi.2020.04.027.

White House Briefing, April 10, 2020. https://www.whitehouse.gov
/briefings-statements/remarks-president-trump-vice-president
-pence-members-coronavirus-task-force-press-briefing-24/.

Wilson, E., and R. R. Callis. *Who Could Afford to Buy a Home in
2009: Affordability of Buying a Home in the United States*. Washington, D.C.: U.S. Census Bureau, 2013. https://www.census
.gov/content/dam/Census/library/publications/2013/demo/h121
_13–02.pdf.

A BOLDER APPROACH TO DIVERSIFY THE HEALTH CARE WORKFORCE

Monica R. McLemore

t no other time in the history of Black people in the United States has there been the current sense of urgency to diversify the health care workforce. The events of 2020 elucidated inconvenient truths long understood by Black America—that clinical health services provision and public health are not prepared to care for us in ways we deserve. Even more frustrating is the fact that our exclusion from the health professions is part of a long history of discrediting and defunding Black people who have aspired to join the professions. Health care hierarchy reinforces this notion, stifles innovative solutions, and unnecessarily keeps us from diversifying the workforce.

Health care hierarchy is defined by how health services are provided within institutions. Hierarchies of health care professionals (e.g., physicians, nurses, pharmacists, etc.) are based on a given job's level of responsibility as determined by funders, professional organizations, policy makers, and regulatory agencies. Health care hierarchy reflects a particular type of structural racism that is explained by segregation. As Dr. Rhea Boyd points out in her 2019 piece in *The Lancet* entitled "The Case for Desegregation":

In health care, most critiques of racial segregation focus on patient segregation, examining how accepted proxies like health insurance status or residential zip codes are used to, in effect, racially segregate patients within and across medical systems. These forms of patient segregation have deleterious effects on health-care quality and patient outcomes. But racial segregation in the health-care workforce, and its relation to population health inequities, remains largely unexamined. This is despite the fact that in the USA, most hospital executives, clinical administrators, medical personnel, public health officials, insurance and pharmaceutical executives, medical educators and tenured faculty, NIH-funded researchers, directors of professional medical associations, and the student pipelines that precede each of these roles are white.

Exclusively funding physicians won't get us to health equity or dismantle health care hierarchy. The 1910 *Flexner Report* represented the most comprehensive landscape analysis (or evaluation) of the caliber and quality of medical schools at the time. There was no consideration of the context in which that care was being provided, particularly the lack of funding, clinical training opportunities, and proper facilities for institutions primarily serving Black people. The report, authored by Abraham Flexner and funded by the Carnegie and Rockefeller Foundations, is widely cited for embodying both the establishment of health care hierarchy and the structural racism of that time, specifically in its lack of policies to support Reconstruction after slavery was abolished.

From the time after the *Flexner Report,* health care hierarchy and structural racism were, and still are, embedded in the evaluation criteria for medical schools and whether they could remain open. For example, the majority of American medical schools that closed, due to the criteria on the *Flexner Report,* served poor people and Black patients. The report and the recommendations contained in it were directly responsible for those closures; it is estimated that if those schools remained open, there would have been almost 180,000 more Black physicians today. It is unknown how many adjacent health professions schools (i.e., nursing, pharmacy, dentistry, midwifery) were also forced to close as a result of the report, and thus, the lack of diversity in the present health care workforce is impossible to quantify.

Further complicating the picture of health care hierarchy and structural racism grounded in policy is gendered racism, the notion that gender oppression and racism intersect for people who embody both identities. Globally, researchers recognize that the health and well-being of our modern world is tied to the health and well-being of women and girls. However, in the U.S., across the reproductive spectrum (e.g., family planning, maternal fetal medicine, reproductive endocrinology and infertility, gynecologic oncology), Black and Brown women and girls have poorer outcomes than their white counterparts. Exposure to gendered racism leads to poor reproductive well-being of women of color, which further narrows the pool of potential scholars—the exact people most likely to have the greatest influence over said outcomes.

Racial discordance between clinical providers, clinician-scholars, and communities has profound implications. Interpersonal processes of care, including social concordance and communication, have been shown to be a significant aspect of quality care. Experiences of care (being treated poorly) has been shown to impact patients' perceptions of the quality of the care they receive, which contributes to mistrust, especially for Black women and people of color. In other words, vaccine hesitancy was a legitimate concern because health care organizations are untrustworthy.

Currently, only 65.6 percent of the U.S. population is white, but 83.2 percent of licensed nurses and 90 percent of certified nurse midwives are white. And while the physician community is more diverse (49 percent white), only 4 percent of physicians are Black or African American. Moreover, there are more Black or African American women physicians (54.7 percent) than men (45.3 percent), but in all other racial and ethnic groups, there are more men than women. There's evidence that shows that 1) people of color in the health professions are more likely to serve minority populations; 2) health care providers who are people of color are more likely to work with publicly insured and minority populations; and 3) programs that provide financial incentives to health care providers who serve minority populations have not been more successful than programs that develop historically excluded health care providers for under-resourced settings. More telling is that data show that white faculty are *unwilling* to diversify their ranks, which has a trickle-down effect particularly at institutions with academic medical centers and graduate health programs. There have been attempts to diversify the clinical health care workforce using incentive and pipeline programs. Incentive programs (where agreement to work in underserved areas affords students opportunities to study without cost) and pipeline programs focus on skill building and career development. Although funded by both the federal government and the private sector, these kinds of programs have had mixed results.

We need a bolder approach to addressing health care hierarchy and structural and gendered racism, which aims to reconcile historical exclusion from the health professions. Three strategies are required to be deployed simultaneously if we are serious about diversifying the future health care workforce.

First, we need new models that test concordance while flattening health care hierarchy. The Black Mamas Matter Alliance is an excellent example of this model where doulas, lawyers, nurses, midwives, physicians, policy experts, and people with lived experience come together as kindred partners—community-based organizations led by Black people—regardless of socioeconomic background. The structure of the alliance supports intergenerational approaches and institutional and organizational capacity and memory.

Second, we need new theoretical models to guide our strategies that include reproductive justice, human rights, and theoretical frameworks that align and connect the clinical determinants of health to the social and structural determinants of health. Recent publications have attempted to infuse antiracism approaches to improving health care, and new guidelines have provided a road map for reimagining the conduct of research with, for, and by Black Mamas, which includes diversification of the health care workforce.

Finally, we need health care reparations, including the investments in the largest producer of science, technology, engineering, mathematics (STEM) and health care graduates at Historically Black Colleges and Universities (HBCUs) from private businesses, philanthropy, publicly traded companies, venture capitalists, and the federal government.

These three approaches are not inclusive of all ideas that could prove successful in the diversification of the health care workforce, nor will they be effective if implemented individually. However, these ideas could collectively provide a strong foundation for moving toward health equity and righting historical wrongs grounded in health care hierarchy and gendered and structural racism. The future deserves a health care workforce that centers and reflects the people most burdened by health disparities—their expertise is vital to any efforts to achieve health equity and improved Black futures.

Works Cited

Black Mamas Matter Alliance. https://blackmamasmatter.org/.

"Black Maternal Health Research Re-Envisioned: Best Practices for the Conduct of Research With, For, and By Black Mamas." *Harvard Law & Policy Review* 14, no. 2 (2020): 393–415. https://harvardlpr.com/wp-content/uploads/sites/20/2020/11/BMMA-Research-Working-Group.pdf.

Boyd, R. W. "The Case for Desegregation." *Lancet* 393, no. 10190 (2019): 2484–2485. doi: 10.1016/S0140–6736(19)31353–4. PMID: 31232362.

"Current Status of the U.S. Physician Workforce." Association of American Colleges of Medicine, 2014. http://www.aamcdiversityfactsandfigures.org/section-ii-current-status-of-us-physician-workforce/index.html.

Davidson, P. M., S. J. McGrath, A. I. Meleis, P. Stern, M. Digiacomo, T. Dharmendra, R. Correa-de-Araujo, et al. "The Health of Women and Girls Determines the Health and Well-Being of our Modern World: A White Paper from the International Council on Women's Health Issues." *Health Care for Women International* 32, no. 10 (2011): 870–886.

Dehlendorf, C., J. T. Henderson, E. Vittinghoff, K. Grumbach, K. Levy, J. Schmittdiel, J. Lee, D. Schillinger, and J. Steinauer. "Association of the Quality of Interpersonal Care During Family Planning Counseling with Contraceptive Use." *American Journal of Obstetrics and Gynecology* 215, no. 1 (2016): 78.e1–e9.

Duffy, T. P. "The Flexner Report—100 Years Later." *Yale Journal of Biology and Medicine* 84, no. 3 (2011): 269–276.

Eichelberger, K. Y., K. Doll, G. E. Ekpo, and M. L. Zerden. "Black Lives Matter: Claiming a Space for Evidence-Based Outrage in

Obstetrics and Gynecology." *American Journal of Public Health* 106, no. 10 (2016): 1771–1772.

Gasman, M. B. "The Five Things No One Will Tell You About Why Colleges Don't Hire More Faculty of Color." Hechinger Report, September 20, 2016. https://hechingerreport.org/five-things-no-one-will-tell-colleges-dont-hire-faculty-color/.

Greenwood, B. N., R. R. Hardeman, L. Huang, and A. Sojourner. "Physician-Patient Racial Concordance and Disparities in Birthing Mortality for Newborns." *Proceedings of the National Academy of Sciences of the United States of America* 117, no. 35 (2020): 21194–21200.

Hlavinka, E. "Racial Bias in Flexner Report Permeates Medical Education Today—Landmark Study Forced All but Two Black U.S. Medical Schools to Close." MedPage Today, June 18, 2020. https://www.medpagetoday.com/publichealthpolicy/medicaleducation/87171. Accessed December 14, 2021.

Kogan, M. D., M. Kotelchuk, G. R. Alexander, and W. E. Johnson. "Racial Disparities in Reported Prenatal Care Advice from Health Care Providers." *American Journal of Public Health* 84 (1994): 82–88.

Missing Persons: Minorities in the Health Professions. n.p.: Sullivan Commission on Diversity in the Health Care Workforce, 2004. Retrieved from http://www.thesullivanalliance.org/cue/research/publications.html.

Paul, D. A., R. Locke, K. Zook, K. H. Leef, J. L. Stefano, and G. Colmorgen. "Racial Differences in Prenatal Care of Mothers Delivering Very Low Birth Weight Infants." *Journal of Perinatology* 26, no. 2 (2006): 74–78.

Rosenthal, L., and M. Lobel. "Gendered Racism and the Sexual and Reproductive Health of Black and Latina Women." *Ethnicity*

& Health, February 2018. Published ahead of print. doi: 10.1080/13557858.2018.1439896.

Thornton, R. L., N. R. Powe, D. Roter, and L. A. Cooper. "Patient-Physician Social Concordance, Medical Visit Communication and Patients' Perceptions of Health Care Quality." *Patient Education and Counseling* 85, no. 3 (2011): e201–e208.

Smith, S. G., P. A. Nsiah-Kumi, P. R. Jones, and R. J. Pamies. "Pipeline Programs in the Health Professions, Part 1: Preserving Diversity and Reducing Health Disparities." *Journal of the National Medical Association* 101, no. 9 (2009): 836–840, 845–851.

Smith, S. G., P. A. Nsiah-Kumi, P. R. Jones, and R. J. Pamies. "Pipeline Programs in the Health Professions, Part 2: The Impact of Recent Legal Challenges to Affirmative Action." *Journal of the National Medical Association* 101, no. 9 (2009): 852–863.

RACE, GENDER, AND RETHINKING CARE WORK

Yolonda Y. Wilson

Thinking seriously about health justice, including ameliorating health disparities, requires centering both the importance of care work and creating policies that support those who disproportionately engage in paid and unpaid caregiving in the U.S. This work is often un- or underpaid and is primarily performed by women. More specifically, women of color, particularly Black women, perform this labor both within families and communities and in the workforce. This un- and underpaid work contributes to the persistence of the wealth gap in the U.S. that is both raced and gendered. As of 2018, Black women earn on average 61.8 cents for every dollar that a white man earns, and the average Black family has a dime of wealth for every dollar that the average white family has. By no means am I suggesting that merely increasing the pay for Black women, especially Black women who engage in care work, would close this wealth gap. Closing this gap will additionally require significant, sustained policy changes, a few of which I will explore below.

For clarity, I use the term *family caregiver* to refer to the unpaid physical and/or emotional labor that family members, friends, neighbors, and community members perform to assist those with chronic illness or disabilities with daily tasks. I use *paid caregiver* to refer to the low-wage, physically and emotionally demanding—and sometimes outright dangerous—labor that workers such as home health aides and nurses' aides perform, often in the homes of people who are not related to them.

As U.S. baby boomers age, the numbers of adults needing care has grown and will continue to grow. Additionally, millions of adults who are not aged need some measure of daily assistance due to chronic illness and/or disability. Family caregivers and paid caregivers face similar challenges, and given the disproportionate clustering of Black women in low-paid, low-status, physically demanding work, many of them occupy the roles of family caregiver and paid caregiver simultaneously. In other words, Black women who disproportionately comprise the ranks of nurses' aides, for example, often find caregiving work awaiting them at home after a long shift of feeding patients, turning patients, emptying bedpans, changing diapers, and physically lifting patients.

As of 2018, the average family caregiver in the U.S. (across race) is a forty-nine-year-old woman who works full-time in addition to family caregiving. The unpaid family caregiving work that women (across race) perform in U.S. households is estimated to be worth approximately $470 billion. Black women in particular bear the brunt of performing this unpaid labor, which means that they are losing significant wages each year. Moreover, Black women are often further disadvantaged economically due to family and paid caregiving responsibilities because career, educational, and other aspirations are put on hold or abandoned entirely due to un- or low-paid care work.

While some argue differences in wages and wealth are the natural cause of women's own decisions to engage in care work, this ignores the broader social expectations that contribute to those decisions and which broader social expectations that any policy pronouncements must consider. One must understand that care work isn't only work but that the "caregiving role" is an example of a social role. Following Ron Mallon, I understand a social role to be

> a particular sort of niche (niche—"a causal role that may
> be occupied by a thing"), distinguished by its occupant
> being acted upon by special sorts of conceptual or
> linguistic causes. Social roles in this sense are part of
> the apparatus that coordinates and structures social life
> within a community.

Social roles are significant not only for the individuals who occupy them but for the entire community in which those individuals live. Social roles are partly responsible for forming the basis, or structure, of social life. They allow members of the community to distinguish the different tasks within the community, as well as to pick out who will be responsible for performing those tasks. Social roles set expectations of the various members of the community. Social roles come with their own internal and external complexities (within communities and within individuals). Individuals within communities and the communities themselves must navigate these complexities. For Black women, this means race and gender operate simultaneously to shape expectations about one's place in a community, what occupations one holds or should hold, and even what one's temperament and values are assumed to be.

The historical roles that Black women have occupied in the labor force, maintained by law and by custom, the continuing discrimination that Black women in the labor market face, and imagery that reinforces who Black women are in the popular imagination have converged to create the social role "Black woman." That many imaginings of Black womanhood are synonymous with caregiving highlights important tensions within social roles: those who occupy a given social role may understand themselves very differently from those members of the community who do not occupy that role. Thus, social pressure, including internally exerted pressure, may influence Black women's decision to engage in both family caregiving and paid caregiving.

The COVID-19 pandemic also revealed the importance of caregivers and how disproportionately vulnerable women of color who perform this work are to illness and injury due to inadequate protections. What remains true is that although Black people are more frequently forced to navigate chronic illness (like diabetes and lupus), we are also experiencing disproportionate degrees of un- and underemployment. As a philosopher-bioethicist, I fundamentally believe that care work is essential work and that health justice includes honoring, acknowledging, and compensating the work of caregivers.

Moving forward, the United States must show proper value for care work and caregivers. First, caregivers must receive a paid, living wage. Some states have provisions to compensate family care work. Through its Paid Family Leave program, California allows individuals, who take time off from work, to receive a share of their wages to care for a family member. Although this is one of the more generous policies currently in the U.S., it fails to address the reality that much of Black women's work in the paid labor force is underpaid, so to the extent that the amount of compensation one is potentially eligible for is not enough to sustain individuals or families. Additionally, one can only take advantage of the state's family leave act for up to eight weeks in a twelve-month period. I propose that the wage be one that sustains individuals and families, lacks time constraints, and becomes federal. Implementing this wage structure can potentially alleviate the burden of trying to navigate care work and other forms of work.

Second, because Black women are likely to forgo educational as well as employment opportunities to engage in care work, Historically Black Colleges and Universities (HBCUs) and other minority-serving institutions (MSIs) should be at the forefront of conversations about supporting Black women's educational aspirations even in the face of the care expectations placed on Black women. Because of their student and employee demographics, HBCUs and MSIs are uniquely positioned to understand the kind of care work that Black women do while attempting to complete degrees.

One may object that I have not addressed the injustice that creates the expectations that Black women fulfill the social role of caregiving in the first place. This is ultimately an important justice goal. At the same time, I am thinking about where the United States is now and what policies could make a difference in the interim while continuing to strive for freedom from the unjust expectations that one will fulfill constricting social roles. Finally, it may be the case that even after these unjust expectations are overcome, there will still be instances where Black women will *want to* engage in care work for any number of reasons. Care work, as essential work, should be valued for its own sake, and the Black women who disproportionately engage in care work should not face further disadvantage as a result of doing the work. In fact, rethinking care work gives us the opportunity to think, not only of increased compensation (which is a must) but also to revamp education and educational opportunities in light of the demands that care work places on Black women.

Works Cited

Broyles, Michaela. "A Conversation About the Racial Wealth Gap and How to Address It." Brookings Institution, June 18, 2019. https://www.brookings.edu/blog/brookings-now/2019/06/18/a -conversation-about-the-racial-wealth-gap-and-how-to-address-it/.

The Female Face of Family Caregiving Fact Sheet. Washington, D.C.: National Partnership for Women and Families, 2018. http:// www.nationalpartnership.org/our-work/resources/workplace /female-face-family-caregiving.pdf.

Hegewisch, Ariane, and Adiam Tesfaselassie. *The Gender Wage Gap: 2018: Earnings Differences by Race, Gender and Ethnicity.* Washington, D.C.: Institute for Women's Policy Research, September 2019. https://iwpr.org/wp-content/uploads/2019/09/C484.pdf.

Mallon, Ron. "Social Construction, Social Roles, and Stability." In *Socializing Metaphysics,* edited by Frederick F. Schmitt. Lanham, MD: Rowman & Littlefield, 2003.

"Paid Family Leave." Employment Development Department, State of California. https://www.edd.ca.gov/disability/paid_family _leave.htm.

PART III

WELLNESS

To health and inequity scholars, the idea that Black Americans live sicker and die younger comes as no surprise, but as a logical result of social realities.

—JAIME SLAUGHTER-ACEY

The Black [WELLNESS] Agenda outlines four health care scenarios that lie at the intersection of race, gender, and class. As noted by Dr. Jaime Slaughter-Acey, racial health disparities in the United States transcend time, place, and outcome. Ongoing racism plays a role in protecting the health status of white people while damaging the health of Black Americans. Historically, health disparities have plagued this nation's ability to provide Black people with adequate health care that aims to serve us at our greatest time of need, and this is especially true for Black Americans who are particularly vulnerable to the system, including, but not limited to, mothers and children, disabled folks, and individuals lacking mental health access.

In 2020, concerns across the United States about the state of wellness became widespread, with everyone from activists to entrepreneurs to athletes joining the conversation. This chapter of the book exists as an extension of the health care chapter, which illustrated ways to address the underlying structural racism within the healthcare system. In this chapter, experts and activists will build on those ideas to describe how the health care system undermines and under-serves the most vulnerable among us and why that needs to change:

- Epidemiologist **Jaime Slaughter-Acey** explains how the conversation surrounding colorism must expand to include how Black mothers and their children are endangered when it comes to the kind of maternal and infant health they receive.

- Disability activist **Tinu Abayomi-Paul** gives a raw account of her experience as a Black disabled woman in America and what policies would best serve those who go through similar experiences. She draws on her own personal narrative to set the stage for how disabled people from marginalized communities should be treated moving forward.

- Health economist **Jevay Grooms** illustrates how unequal access to mental health services harms Black people disproportionately and why prioritizing said access will make a difference for Black America as a whole.

- **Ashlee Wisdom,** cofounder of Health In Her HUE, a digital platform that connects Black women to culturally sensitive health care providers, health content, and community, argues for how technology can be used to provide access to wellness services catered specifically to Black women and the needs of women of color more broadly.

WHY COLORISM MATTERS FOR
BLACK MATERNAL AND INFANT HEALTH

Jaime Slaughter-Acey

n 2018, *New York Times Magazine* author Linda Villarosa brought renewed attention to a very old problem with an article entitled "Why America's Black Mothers and Babies Are in a Life or Death Crisis." Villarosa correctly answered this question with the observation that it "has everything to do with the lived experiences of being a Black woman in America."

To health and inequity scholars, the idea that Black Americans live sicker and die younger comes as no surprise but as a logical result of social realities. Racial health disparities in the United States transcend time, place, and outcome. Historical, contemporary, and intergenerational racism play a fundamental role in protecting the health status of whites while damaging the health status of Black Americans.

Black women in the United States are two to three times more likely to experience pregnancy-related complications or death compared to their racial/ethnic counterparts. Additionally, one in every seven Black infants is born too soon (prior to thirty-seven week's gestation) and faces an infant mortality rate that is triple the infant mortality rate of preterm infants born to white mothers. Black women in the United States and their babies have carried the disproportionate burden of poor maternal and infant health outcomes since before the routine recording of national vital statistics began in the early 1900s.

Maternal and infant health for Black women and their infants is impeded by U.S. reproductive politics that minimize women's autonomy over their bodies, reproductive choice, and access to reproductive health care. The injustice that ensues, however, is not distributed equally across all Black women. Health disparities research in recent years has in fact considered colorism in addition to racism as one of the fundamental drivers of the maternal and infant health epidemic in this country.

Colorism, also called *skin tone bias,* is a phenotype-based system of oppression that endows privilege and opportunity to people based on the hue of their skin, bequeaths privilege to individuals with lighter skin tones and more Eurocentric phenotypic characteristics over individuals with darker complexions and more Afrocentric attributes. As a spin-off of cultural racism—beliefs in the supremacy of whiteness that are enmeshed in the cultural values and norms of societal institutions, ideology, and the everyday actions of individuals—colorism operates across multiple social contexts and settings while modifying exposure to and the embodiment of systemic racism.

Beyond the patterning of education and economic opportunities (predictors of maternal and infant health), scholars find skin color is associated with one's exposure to experiences of discrimination and stress. To buffer against the effects of discrimination and other structural and psychosocial stressors, individuals can draw from psychosocial resources linked to maternal health and well-being, such as self-esteem, mastery, racial identity, and socialization.

Black women in the United States face multiple and simultaneous sources of chronic stress, stigma, and discrimination that are tied to their gender, status as racial/ethnic minorities, and skin color. An emerging body of scholarship finds colorism may have more consequential effects on the health of America's Black women than men, through the deleterious impact of maternal health care.

If we are to address the long-standing racial disparities in maternal and infant health outcomes that have plagued this country since before its founding, we must address the social meaning of skin color and its intersection with race. Racism is part and parcel of Black Americans' daily lived experiences that extend over a life span. From cradle to grave, racism protects the health status of whites and damages the health status of Black Americans. As a system and process, racism structures economic, political, social, and ideological opportunity. It also assigns value to interpersonal exchanges based on perceived or assigned race, which is reinforced by skin color, our most visible physical attribute.

For the United States to be a safe place to give birth for all women, the maternal health of the Black woman, "our essential mother," in the words of Alice Walker's *In Search of Our Mothers' Gardens,* must be valued. Her life and the life of her child must be treated with care and respect. Thankfully, Black-led maternal and child health organizations—like SisterSong and Black Mamas Matter—are leading this charge to address the shortcomings of U.S. reproductive politics and health care. Investment in maternal health data collection, ensuring access to doulas during childbirth, investment in community-based health care in Black communities, and extending Medicaid coverage from sixty days postpartum to a full year after childbirth are just a few of the policies that will begin to support and promote Black maternal health.

Works Cited

Ely, D. M., and A. K. Driscoll. "Infant Mortality in the United States, 2017: Data from the Period Linked Birth/Infant Death File." *National Vital Statistics Report* Vol. 69, no. 7 (2020).

Haines, Michael. "Fertility and Mortality in the United States." EH.Net Encyclopedia, Robert Whaples, ed. March 19, 2008. URL http://eh.net/encyclopedia/fertility-and-mortality-in-the -united-states/.

Cooper Owens, Deirdre, and Sharla M. Fett. "Black Maternal and Infant Health: Historical Legacies of Slavery." *American Journal of Public Health* Vol.109 (10) (2019): 1342–1345. ISSN: 0090–0036 , 1541–0048; DOI: 10.2105/AJPH.2019.305243.

Jones, J. "Constructing Race and Deconstructing Racism: A Cultural Psychology Approach." *Handbook of Racial & Ethnic Minority Psychology,* Bernai G., Trimble, J., Burlew A., eds. Thousand Oaks, CA: SAGE Publications, Inc., 2003: 276–290. 10.4135/9781412976008.n14.

Keith, V. M., A. W. Nguyen, R. J. Taylor, D. M. Mouzon, and L. M. Chatters. "Microaggressions, Discrimination, and Pheno-type among African Americans: A Latent Class Analysis of the Impact of Skin Tone and BMI." *Sociological Inquiry* 87 (2017): 233–255.

Monk, E. P., Jr. "The Cost of Color: Skin Color, Discrimination, and Health among African-Americans." *American Journal of Sociology* 121 (2015): 396–444.

Singh, G. K. "Trends and Social Inequalities in Maternal Mortality in the United States, 1969–2018." *International Journal of Maternal and Child Health and AIDS (IJMA),* 10(1), (2020): 29–42.

Singh, G. K., and Stella M. Yu. "Infant Mortality in the United States, 1915–2017: Large Social Inequalities Have Persisted for over a Century." *International Journal of Maternal and Child Health and AIDS,* 8(1), 19 (2019).

Slaughter-Acey, J. C., D. Sneed, L. Parker, V. M. Keith, N. L. Lee, and D. P. Misra. "Skin Tone Matters: Racial Microaggressions and Delayed Prenatal Care." *American Journal of Preventive Medicine* 57 (2019): 321–329.

Thompson, M. S., and V. M. Keith. "The Blacker the Berry: Gender, Skin Tone, Self-Esteem, and Self-Efficacy." *Gender and Society* 15 (2001): 336-357.

Uzogara, E. E., and J. S. Jackson. "Perceived Skin Tone Discrimination Across Contexts: African American Women's Reports." *Race and Social Problems* 8 (2016): 147–159.

THE DIARY OF A BLACK DISABLED WOMAN

Tinu Abayomi-Paul

To be a Black disabled woman in America is to be unwillingly invisible in your greatest time of need. The most visible layer as a Black disabled person is our Blackness, which is constantly under the threat of scrutiny, assumed guilt, and, as logically follows, persecution.

Our pain isn't taken seriously, as is borne out by multiple studies as well as my own experience of chronic pain. We are believed to be able to bear more pain. Some medical devices don't work as well for us due to our skin color. These compounding issues of racism, sexism, and ableism endanger the lives of Black disabled women.

At this point, there are two basic things that disabled people and chronically ill people don't have—upward mobility in alignment with our ability to work and access to proper health care. As a disabled person, you can never be sure you received proper care. Navigating what this country calls a health care system is difficult. If you need to see a specialist, which most chronically ill or disabled people do, you have to go through paperwork or related delays. Then there's everything before the appointment: setting the appointment in coordination with related testing and arranging transportation.

To add insult to injury, disabling conditions can and have

contributed to lack of access to equal employment opportunities, which Black people already do not have access to; this can get more complicated for those of us whose symptoms or disabilities aren't apparent by looking at us. Essentially, thousands of eligible people each month die waiting for benefits. And if you're lucky enough to get them? We are pretty much taking a vow of poverty, as our ability to acquire assets and generate an income is limited by our disability.

Moving forward, policy makers need to recognize that health care is a human right and not a privilege afforded to those who can afford it. Having affordable or universal health care for all would be a simple way to help solve the problem of chronically ill and disabled people being treated better, partly because being able to fully afford care would stabilize many of us. Even more would not develop the additional conditions that result from not being able to receive stable or proper treatment.

The Centers for Disease Control and Prevention's *Guideline for Prescribing Opioids for Chronic Pain,* for example, has made it incredibly difficult for pain patients to receive treatment (that is fifty million Americans who used to be able to live and work, albeit in relative discomfort, left in pain). While there is a problem with opiate overdoses, restricting prescriptions has not decreased the rate of overdose and addiction. That's because, despite exciting television plots, overprescribing hasn't been the problem with opiates since the mid-2010s. The problem now is illegal fentanyl being sold to desperate people who try to get their medication without going through the proper channels.

Being better served in health care also means listening to

disabled people. Health care facilities could hire various types of chronically ill and disabled people to give feedback in all areas. It's hard to see what we need if no one asks us.

We're often uncomfortable in pharmacies and waiting rooms, made to stand in line. Meanwhile, the system of taking a number seems to work well in delis, butcher shops, or motor vehicle departments. Moreover, we often don't get the services we need until nondisabled people need them. We have asked for video doctor appointments and telehealth long before the pandemic, but once the rest of the world needed them, they became commonplace quickly.

The problem of the perception of Black disabled women is a long-standing one. It's complicated by intersectionality—we aren't a monolithic group with a one-size-fits-all solution. But if the world doesn't treat white women with the same cookie-cutter approach, why do that for Black women?

With respect to generating access to equitable health care, especially for Black women, part of the answer is self-evident. The recent victories of women like Stacey Abrams, Serena and Venus Williams, Kamala Harris, and the endless list of Black women who excel, some with disabilities, show the world what we already know: that Black women can lead. And so we should let Black women lead, unencumbered, with respect to assisting in equitable health care services for disabled people. Putting more Black women in charge would not be an act of charity. The economy has lost $16 trillion due to racism, so it's hard to avoid the conclusion that subverting racism would be profitable.

Being put in charge isn't the only resolution here. As a Black disabled woman, I would not have to worry about being well enough to work if I could receive the proper accommodations to apply for jobs and still be considered fairly. Thus, workplace accommodations should be the norm and enforced by law.

Begin by including accommodations in job listings. So many job descriptions say that they require sitting, standing, lifting, or driving, but in practice, the majority of those jobs could easily be performed without any of these restrictions. Currently, there's not enough enforcement of the Americans with Disabilities Act (ADA), and if there were, there's a huge loophole in it called *undue hardship*. If a business can claim that accommodating a disabled person would be too expensive or cumbersome, they can claim undue hardship, which means no accommodation for disabled people or people with chronic illness.

As a small business owner myself, I understand why these guidelines are in place. But perhaps instead of having a loophole that allows businesses not to help disabled people work comfortably, there should be programs that incentivize businesses to remove the obstacles that prevent disabled people from being able to work. The Small Business Administration could be incentivized to fund businesses that are making efforts to hire and serve disabled employees and customers.

Finally, it must be understood that disabled people don't have "special needs." We just have needs that, like everyone else's, differ from person to person. Giving them a separate name makes it sound like we're being given something extra. Then when it comes time for legislation to help change our circumstances, the perception hurts our chances of success. Yes, it is possible that, in the workplace, we may need better chairs, but wouldn't this change benefit all employees?

Give us, the chronically ill, mentally ill, disabled, neurodivergent, deaf, or blind, the same things, beginning with access to proper health care and opportunities for upward mobility in alignment with our ability to work.

Disabled people want the things the rest of the world takes for granted. While it would make life a bit more boring than what we are used to, we would rather be treated as regular people, allowed to fully thrive.

Works Cited

"About CDC's Opioid Prescribing Guideline." Centers for Disease Control and Prevention. https://www.cdc.gov/drugoverdose /prescribing/guideline.html.

Akala, A. "NPR Cookie Consent and Choices." NPR, September 23, 2020. https://www.npr.org/sections/live-updates-protests -for-racial-justice/2020/09/23/916022472/cost-of-racism-u-s -economy-lost-16-trillion-because-of-discrimination-bank-says.

Crenshaw, Kimberlé. "She Coined the Term 'Intersectionality' Over 30 Years Ago. Here's What It Means to Her Today." *Time,* February 20, 2020. https://time.com/5786710/kimberle-crenshaw -intersectionality/.

Feiner, J. R., J. W. Severinghaus, and P. E. Bickler. "Dark Skin Decreases the Accuracy of Pulse Oximeters at Low Oxygen Saturation: The Effects of Oximeter Probe Type and Gender." *Anesthesia & Analgesia* 105, no. 6 (2007 suppl): S18–S23. doi: 10.1213/01.ane.0000285988.35174.d9. PMID: 18048893.

Joyner, Jazmine. "Nobody Believes That Black Women Are in Pain, and It's Killing Us." Wear Your Voice, May 24, 2018. https:// wearyourvoicemag.com/black-women-are-in-pain.

Picchi, A. "Almost 110,000 Americans Died While Waiting for a Social Security Disability Hearing." CBS News. https://www .cbsnews.com/amp/news/disability-benefits-gao-report-death -bankruptcies-waiting-hearings/.

Rao, Vidya. "Implicit Bias in Medicine: How It Hurts Black Women." Today, July 27, 2020. https://www.today.com/health /implicit-bias-medicine-how-it-hurts-black-women-t187866.

Rulli, L., and J. Leckerman, J. "Unfinished Business: The Fading Promise of ADA Enforcement in the Federal Courts Under Title

I and Its Impact on the Poor." *Journal of Gender, Race & Justice* 8 (2005): 595. https://scholarship.law.upenn.edu/cgi/viewcontent .cgi?article=1675&context=faculty_scholarship.

Stallings, Erika. "This Is How the American Health Care System Is Failing Black Women." Oprah Daily, October 6, 2020. https:// www.oprahmag.com/life/health/a23100351/racial-bias-in-health care-black-women.

"Undue Hardship." Thomson Reuters Practical Law. https://content.next.westlaw.com/2–504–2937 ?transitionType=Default&contextData=(sc.Default)&__ lrTS=20190126185658646&firstPage=true.

MENTAL HEALTH FOR BLACK AMERICA

Jevay Grooms

n 2019, there were 51.5 million adults in the United States with mental illness. According to the survey, half of white adults with mental illness received services compared to just a third of Black adults. Modern treatments for mental illness in the United States have evolved from institutionalizing individuals to managing conditions with the use of community agencies, including trained social workers and mental health counselors. With changes in mental health treatment has come a better understanding of the needs of the 21 percent of Americans adults who suffer from mental illness. Yet as with many aspects of everyday life, the mental health treatment of Black Americans lags behind that of their white counterparts.

Of the many factors that impact utilization rates of mental health services, one often-cited reason for not seeking medical treatment, in general, is the lack of health insurance or financial means to cover the costs associated with treatment. The Affordable Care Act (ACA) aimed to help alleviate this barrier. In 2010, the ACA, also known as Obamacare, established behavioral health as one of the ten essential health benefits that must be covered by individual and small group health insurance plans. In my recent coauthored paper focused on Medicaid admissions as a measure of access for substance use disorder

(SUD) treatment, I find that the enactment of the ACA is associated with an increase in Medicaid admission for SUDs among Black, white, and Native American admissions. As a mental health researcher, I find it rewarding to see behavioral health ailments of all types, substance use disorders included, getting the social and clinical acknowledgment they deserve. While mental health treatment is more accessible today than in prior decades, mental health services remain inaccessible to many Black Americans.

Prior to the 2014 expansion of Medicaid, it was estimated that 72 percent of white nonelderly Americans received health coverage from an employer or private source compared to 46 percent of Black Americans. Additionally, as of 2020, fourteen states have yet to expand Medicaid, seven of which are overrepresented Black—that is, they have a more substantial percentage of Black residents than the U.S. population, 13.4 percent. This echoes similar results coauthors and I discussed in a Brookings Institution blog post. Using a unique nationally represented survey, the National Panel Study of COVID-19 (NPSC-19), fielded in the spring of 2020 during the coronavirus pandemic, we found Black and Hispanic essential non–health care workers reported no health insurance coverage four times more often than white essential non–health care workers. This was particularly disconcerting given the elevated risk of exposure frontline workers incur during the pandemic.

In current research with Alberto Ortega, Joaquin Rubalcaba, and Edward Vargas, we use data from the aforementioned survey to assess American households' well-being through the pandemic with a particular interest in vulnerable populations: Black households, Hispanic households, low-income households, and households headed by essential non–health care workers. In a paper that resulted from a wave of this survey field in April 2020 with over 3,300 respondents, we investigated mental health distress across race, ethnicity, and employment during the pandemic. On average, all Americans surveyed reported elevated levels of mental health distress. More importantly, our analysis illustrates that Black and Hispanic essential non–health care workers had significant and substantial levels of heightened mental health distress relative to white respondents across all measures. Furthermore, we find that for nearly all the inventories, Black respondents report significantly elevated levels of mental health distress as compared to their white counterparts across all worker classifications studied—nonessential, essential non–health care, and essential health care.

These findings are of particular importance given past research finds that, on average, racial and ethnic minorities underreport mental health distress. Thus, if we begin to observe increased reporting from minorities, medical professionals and the health care system need to be prepared to address some of the other factors that contribute to disparities in mental health care, such as lack of insurance, lower-quality care, and cultural incompetency. While ongoing research on the pandemic illuminates the looming mental health crises all Americans face as a result of measures taken to minimize the effect and spread of coronavirus, a particular interest needs to be placed on subsets of the American population who have historically and traditionally been undertreated for mental health ailments.

The elevated levels of mental health distress also raise concerns regarding the co-occurrence of mental illness and substance use disorders. While directionality is less clear, several national surveys have estimated that roughly half of individuals who experience any mental illness in their lifetimes will also have a SUD. Prior to the passage of the ACA, SUD treatment was not covered under all health insurance plans. Of the plans under which it was, a significant portion had a limit on the number of visits, while others lumped mental health and SUD visits under the same umbrella, forcing patients to choose which ailment to treat, as only one was covered. This was true for private insurance and to some extent public insurance, as Medicaid was regulated at the state level. Including SUD treatment in the ACA was imperative to ensure that individuals who suffer from SUDs have access to immediate care, as well as treatment for the myriad of comorbidities, which could persist even after the discontinued use of substances.

The contrast of the national reaction to the opioid epidemic and the crack cocaine epidemic should give pause to all of America, not just Black communities. Those over thirty-five years of age are old enough to remember firsthand the scare tactics that society and all levels of government used when discussing the crack cocaine epidemic. The "war on drugs" marked a period marred with stringent sentencing and vehement drug criminalization, which put a disproportionate percentage of impoverished Black people behind bars. This is in glaring contrast with the much more compassionate response to the prescription opioid epidemic, which emphasized the importance of treatment. Yet it is unclear whether mistakes of the past will be rectified.

In recent research, Alberto Ortega and I assess trends in admissions and completion of SUD treatment and find Black substance users are significantly less likely to complete treatment and more likely to be terminated from treatment than white substance users. We also uncover some evidence suggesting that Black substance users of the past never received the proper medical treatment to address their mental health needs. Thus, we observe admissions for cocaine / crack cocaine among Black patients over fifty years old are three times higher than that of white patients of the same age.

For most of America, being wealthier, more educated, or moving to a neighborhood with better medical care can directly lead to more desirable health outcomes. For Black Americans, this is not necessarily the case. What are often deemed social determinants of health for other demographics will not always lead to better care for Black Americans due to racism, whether explicit or implicit, individual or structural. Thus, it is essential to ensure that preexisting barriers in seeking mental health treatment do not further exacerbate the prevailing disparities in diagnosis and treatment of mental illnesses.

The American Psychological Association estimates that half of all the prison and jail population suffer from mental illness, a population that is 40 percent Black. It is nearly impossible for inmates to seek treatment while incarcerated, and efforts to reduce racial biases in policing and sentencing must be made in order to lower exposure to the additional psychological impact of prison. Additionally, efforts such as Ban the Box, which focus on rehabilitation, should be geared toward behavioral health treatment.

The mental health of Black America has yet to be made a priority, but one might expect this given the disparities in health care more generally. The prevalence of racial and ethnic differences in morbidity, mortality, access to medical care, and health care quality are well documented, and such disparities persist even after controlling for socioeconomic conditions. As a nation, it is imperative that we place the mental health of all people at the forefront of their medical treatment. It must also be acknowledged that Black America has a greater need for services that have been withheld or inadequately provided for decades. Unfortunately, treating the mental health of Black America cannot happen in a vacuum. While increasing access to mental health services is important, and the 2010 expansion of Medicaid and the legislating of essential health benefits as part of the ACA have made a significant impact, they have not and will not solve the centuries-long issues of systemic and institutional racism that still proliferate in everyday life for Black America.

Works Cited

The AFCARS Report, No. 6: Interim FY 1999 Estimates. Washington, DC: U.S. DHHS, Children's Bureau, n.d.

Artiga, S., K. Orgera, and A. Damico. "Changes in Health Coverage by Race and Ethnicity Since the ACA, 2010–2018." Kaiser Family Foundation. Retrieved March 5, 2020. https://www.kff .org/racial-equity-and-health-policy/issue-brief/changes-in-health -coverage-by-race-and-ethnicity-since-the-aca-2010–2018/.

Bharadwa, P., M. M. Pai, and A. Suziedelyte. "Mental Health Stigma." *Economics Letters* 159 (2017): 57–60.

Fiscella, K., P. Franks, M. Gold, and C. Clancy. "Inequality in Quality: Addressing Socioeconomic, Racial, and Ethnic Disparities in Health Care." *JAMA* 283, no. 19 (2000): 2579–2584.

Garcia, J. Nadine. "Remembering Margaret Heckler's Commitment to Advancing Minority Health." *Health Affairs* (blog), November 16, 2018.

Grooms, J., and A. Ortega. "Getting with the Program: Medicaid Expansion and Access to Substance Use Treatment." Working paper.

Grooms, J., and A. Ortega. "Substance Use Disorders Among Older Populations: What Role Does Race and Ethnicity Play in Treatment and Completion?" *Journal of Substance Abuse Treatment* (forthcoming).

Grooms, J., A. Ortega, and J. Rubalcaba. "The COVID-19 Public Health and Economic Crises Leave Vulnerable Populations Exposed." *Hamilton Project* (blog), August 13, 2020.

Grooms, J., A. Ortega, J. Rubalcaba, and E. Vargas. "Racial and Ethnic Disparities: Essential Workers, Mental Health, and the Coronavirus Pandemic." *Review of Black Political Economy* (forthcoming).

Roberts, M. T., E. N. Reither, and S. Lim. "Contributors to Wisconsin's Persistent Black-White Gap in Life Expectancy." *BMC Public Health* 19, no. 891 (2019). https://doi.org/10.1186/s12889-019-7145-y.

Smedley, B. D., A. Y. Stith, and A. R. Nelson. *Unequal Treatment: Confronting Racial and Ethnic Disparities in Health Care.* Washington, D.C.: National Academies Press, 2003.

2019 National Survey on Drug Use and Health (NSDUH). Rockville, MD: Substance Abuse and Mental Health Services Administration, 2020.

U.S. Population Estimates by Age, Sex, Race, and Hispanic Origin: 1980 to 1999. Washington, D.C.: U.S. Census Bureau, 2001.

TECHNOLOGY IS NOT THE PANACEA
FOR BLACK WOMEN'S HEALTH

Ashlee Wisdom

The disparities in health outcomes for Black women have been rigorously studied, well documented, and well reported. They are stark: Black women are three to four times more likely to die from pregnancy-related complications than white women, more likely to die from breast cancer, and more likely to be diagnosed with diabetes and heart disease. This is a direct result of the health inequities caused by structural racism that are pervasive in the U.S.

If you talk to five Black women, at least one of them will tell you their personal experience of feeling unheard, dismissed, or discriminated against by a health care provider. In addition to provider bias, Black women are also constantly bombarded with alarming and triggering headlines about our impending morbidity or premature mortality. But what good is hyper-awareness of a problem without any solutions to address the problem, or, at the very least, solutions to help us better navigate an inequitable health care system? The time has come for health care professionals, researchers, and policy makers to move past a mere willingness to understand health inequities and disparities, toward meaningful action to abolish them.

The U.S. health care system was built on the bodies of Black women, but not designed for Black women. Black women's

bodies have long been experimented on to advance the practice of medicine. Dr. J. Marion Sims, who was named "the
father of gynecology," earned this name by experimenting on
enslaved Black women. Henrietta Lacks was a Black woman
whose cancer cells are the source of the HeLa cell line, the first
immortalized human cell line and one of the most important
cell lines in medical research. Today, work done with the HeLa
cells has been involved in key discoveries in many fields,
including cancer, immunology, and infectious disease. In fact,
one of their most recent applications has been in research for
vaccines against COVID-19. These are only a couple of examples of Black women's bodies being used to advance the study
and practice of medicine. Despite this, Black women still fare
worse on many health outcomes because these advances were
not made to directly benefit them. Furthermore, the legacy of
health care institutions are not well equipped to meet the specific and nuanced health care needs of Black women. They
must become equipped if they truly intend to better serve us,
first and foremost by adopting innovative solutions that are designed *for* and *by* Black women.

As a result of the intersection of racism, sexism, and the
many other isms Black women face, we usually aren't building
nice-to-have solutions. We are usually building intentional, inclusive, and urgent necessities. That was, at least, the case for
me. By 2018, I had read enough papers, reports, and articles
and had enough data to validate what I already knew from
my experience being a Black woman in the U.S. and a Black
woman navigating and working in the U.S. health care system.
Recognizing that it was time to move beyond *understanding*
the problem of racial health disparities, I launched my start-up
Health In Her HUE to connect Black women to culturally com-

petent health care providers, health content, and community. As Toni Morrison put it, "I [got] angry about things and got to work." While I continue to be dismayed by the existing disparities in health outcomes for Black women, I am cautiously optimistic for what the future holds for Black women's health because of the power and potential of technology—that is, technology that is developed and implemented equitably. Recently, we are beginning to see bold innovators building with equity at the center of their solutions. Gone are the days of merely opining about health care issues and using data just for awareness. We are in a technological era where data is now being used to build and drive solutions, and Black women like Toyin Ajayi (Cityblock Health), Nzinga Harrison (Eleanor Health), Simmone Taitt (Poppy Seed Health), Kimberly Seals Allers (Irth), Ivelyse Andino (Radical Health), Melissa Hanna (Mahmee), Sheena Franklin (K'ept Health) are rolling up their sleeves. In addition to these venture- and foundation-backed solutions that Black women are building, technology writ large has significant potential to help close gaps in access, to better engage patients in their care, and allow for better coordination and continuity of care.

The consumerization of health care has completely challenged the status quo of legacy health care institutions. Patients are no longer accepting of the information asymmetry they were conditioned to in the past. They expect a more consumer-friendly health care experience. As long as the United States continues to treat health care like a commodity and not a right, patients deserve to get their care in the way that best meets their needs and preferences.

The expectation for consumer-driven care has led to more innovation in health care, with better provider directories and matching tools, remote patient monitoring solutions for monitoring and supporting patients post-hospital discharge, culturally tailored health content and patient communities, and AI/automation all being leveraged to make health care more efficient and personalized. These developments do not come without issues. The health care system was built on a foundation of racism, and that foundation has yet to be dismantled. Technology, therefore, must be developed in a way that either disrupts or dismantles current systems and structures that are, at worst, failing the most vulnerable patients and, at best, costing us too much money. Innovating solutions without considering systemic racism will only perpetuate and augment existing disparities for Black women, ultimately costing us our lives.

If health technology is going to truly move the needle on health disparities for Black women, it has to consider our lived experiences and social context. What good is technology if it is not accessible, engaging, or meaningfully beneficial to the targeted end user? We also need to reframe the narrative that all solutions targeted to Black women need to be low-tech to be accessible. Black women come from a variety of socioeconomic backgrounds, and irrespective of our socioeconomic status, we are all dealing with health disparities. Yes, innovators do need to consider the digital divide as we think about digital health and health technology. However, I would argue that instead of assuming Black women don't have access to smartphones, broadband, or cell phone data, we should challenge ourselves to examine why we accept pervasive inequality in a technologically advanced society.

I am hopeful that the current tailwinds with respect to COVID-19 and the long-overdue racial reckoning will make room for more radical reimagination and innovation of health care for Black women. COVID-19 has laid bare how health inequities that lead to disparities do none of us any good. I hope we don't get back to a state where acknowledging and normalizing the status quo feels like progress. I hope we continue to feel anxiety around what we will continue to lose if we choose not to innovate, build, and fund solutions on behalf of Black women, especially those being built by Black women. We must work together for a better future for Black women who continue to show up for America time and time again.

Works Cited

"Henrietta Lacks: Science Must Right a Historical Wrong." *Nature* 585, no. 7823 (2020): 7. doi: 10.1038/d41586-020-02494-z.

"Leading Causes of Death—Non-Hispanic Black Females—United States, 2016." Centers for Disease Control and Prevention, September 27, 2019. Accessed July 23, 2021. https://www.cdc.gov /women/lcod/2016/nonhispanic-black/index.htm.

NPR, Robert Wood Johnson Foundation, and Harvard T. H. Chan School of Public Health. *Discrimination in America: Experiences and Views of American Women.* Princeton, NJ: Robert Wood Johnson Foundation, 2017. https://www.rwjf.org/content/dam /farm/reports/surveys_and_polls/2017/rwjf441994.

Tucker, M. J., C. J. Berg, W. M. Callaghan, and J. Hsia. "The Black-White Disparity in Pregnancy-Related Mortality from 5 Conditions: Differences in Prevalence and Case-Fatality Rates." *American Journal of Public Health* 97, no. 2 (2007): 247–251. doi:10.2105/AJPH.2005.072975.

Zhang, S. "The Surgeon Who Experimented on Slaves." *Atlantic,* April 18, 2018. https://www.theatlantic.com/health/archive /2018/04/j-marion-sims/558248/.

PART IV

EDUCATION

Racism, specifically white supremacy in the United States, is at the root of educational inequality in America.
—CARYCRUZ BUENO AND CRUZ CARIDAD BUENO

The Black [EDUCATION] Agenda outlines the trajectory of support, or lack thereof, that young Black people receive throughout their academic and professional journey. As noted by Dr. Carycruz Bueno, the inequities within the education system rob Black students of opportunity. With that in mind, the disruption to schooling across all levels of education in 2020 posed particular challenges for Black students across the nation, as well as students of all races, ethnicities, and nationalities. Educators, administrators, and policy makers alike debated what action steps needed to be taken to ensure that a pandemic bent on disrupting our lives would not in turn put a stop to learning in the classroom. As a result, many discussions came to the forefront, including perspectives from psychologists, economists, professors, and policy makers:

- Economists **Carycruz Bueno** and **Cruz Caridad Bueno** on the considerations of virtual schooling with respect to racial inequality in K–12 classrooms. Based on their own work, they make a case for how structural racism continues to undermine the classroom and how the reconsideration of educational environments due to COVID-19 provides an opportunity for much-needed change.

- Educational psychologist and former assistant director

of the White House Initiative on Educational Excellence for African Americans, **Lauren Mims,** illustrates how expectations that Black girls oftentimes have for themselves in school depends on their instructors. She uses this backdrop to advocate for ways to protect Black girls in the classroom and beyond.

- Early-childhood education researchers **S. Mia Obiwo** and **Francheska Starks** draw on past research studies and contemporary stories centering Black children to advocate for more representation in children's books, and the power of Black characters in shaping Black children's identities.

- Former HBCU business school dean and Brookings fellow **Kristen Broady** reflects on the impact automation will have on how Black college students are trained. Her essay cites Historically Black Colleges and Universities as one way to meet the upcoming challenges and demand of the future labor market.

- Public policy professor **Fenaba Addo** weighs in on the ongoing student debt debate by utilizing her own findings to illustrate how student debt is not just a problem for higher education but also for wealth building.

HOW TO CENTER BLACK CHILDREN DURING A GLOBAL PANDEMIC

Carycruz M. Bueno and Cruz Caridad Bueno

Prior to the pandemic, it was estimated that, on average, for every $2,227 in school funding received by students in predominantly white school districts, students in non-white districts on average received $1 in funding. In addition to funding, inequalities include access to quality prekindergarten, quality teachers, quality facilities, advanced course offerings, among other resources. These are the same inequalities the USA has been tackling since 1966, or the year after *Brown v. Board of Education.* The pandemic and its mismanagement by the federal government has exposed and brought these racial education inequalities to the forefront, and it is only through enacting progressive policies that we can eradicate them.

Racial discrimination in the educational system and the racial educational gap not only pose a problem for the Black community but also create a national economic and security crisis for the country. We know that increases in investment in health and education are the basis of a nation's economic growth. As we move toward a Black and Brown majority in the U.S., failing to provide quality education and opportunities to underserved communities can lead to stagnating or falling economic growth and the perpetuation of low-income work that erodes at the tax-base for the provision of vital government services.

It is imperative to address racial educational inequality for the collective societal and individual well-being of all Americans.

Correcting for racial inequality in education and accompanying adverse societal impacts means that the federal government must expand school choice in a way that eradicates racial inequality. In the 1990s, the conservative solution to educational inequalities was *school choice,* funded with public dollars. School choice theoretically provides all families, regardless of the public neighborhood zoned school, with options, including vouchers for private schools, busing students to other public schools, and charter schools. Although some high-quality charter schools have shown positive impact on inner-city students, school choice itself has been insufficient to eradicate education inequalities. The newest option in school choice is full-time virtual charter schools predominantly run by for-profit organizations and paid for with taxpayer dollars. Research prior to the COVID-19 pandemic shows that students attending full-time virtual charter schools fare worse in standard educational testing, resulting in educational losses akin to one to two years of schooling loss.

COVID-19 has pushed students into full-time virtual schooling without the resources and the infrastructure necessary to address both preexisting educational inequality and the documented detrimental outcomes of virtual learning. Black and Brown students are more likely to live in multigenerational households, meaning they often have less dedicated study space. They are also less likely to have devices and high-speed internet in their households, essential materials to access online education. Given that full-time virtual schools and remote learning were needed to protect the health and lives of all school staff, that it is some families' preferred choice, and the existing research on the negative impacts of virtual school on student achievement, we recommend prioritizing targeted interventions that can help mitigate the negative impact of this school option for the most vulnerable students: Black, Indigenous, and Latino students; students with disabilities; English Language learners; and students from low-income families. Such interventions could consist of high-quality tutoring, more engaging software, ensuring all students have devices and internet, and improving student engagement.

Many of these interventions have been started in different districts, but a larger investment by the federal government is needed to break the poverty cycle. In a post-COVID-19 America, these interventions will help mitigate the learning loss experienced by the most impacted. In addition, there must be discussion and debate about the use of taxpayer dollars to pay for virtual schools run by for-profit organizations when research shows they underperform with regard to both students' cognitive and behavioral outcomes when compared to public schools.

Moreover, there are policies that have been recommended before COVID-19 that still stand to help. First, more funding is required for resources for low-income and Black students. Research finds that a 10 percent increase in per-student spending for twelve years leads to 9.6 percent higher wages and reduces the incidence of adult poverty by 6.1 percentage points. Second, we must ensure a more diverse teacher workforce, specifically more Black and Brown teachers. Dr. Constance Lindsay finds that when Black students have a Black teacher, they are less likely to receive exclusionary discipline. This has important implications for moving students away from the punitive school-to-prison pipeline mentality to one of engaging and transformative learning. Third, we must call for more teacher training on implicit bias toward Black students to improve various outcomes, such as perception, discipline, and recommending for advanced course offerings. Francis (2012) shows that Black girls are perceived to be more disruptive and less likely to get recommended to upper-level math classes by their teachers; a crucial disparity, as these courses are our gateways to high-paying jobs in industries such as economics, engineering, and computer science. Fourth, the government must require true racial school integration, which, to date, has not been achieved. There is evidence from the 1970s and 1980s that suggests that students who attended well-integrated and well-funded schools versus those who didn't fared better with respect to social mobility. Finally, a culturally responsive and social justice curriculum must be implemented, focusing on anti-Black racism, inclusive American history, and dismantling structural inequalities in all schools for all students.

The United States' education system is built on racist foundations and policies. We need to address structural racism across the health, labor, and housing market in conjunction with the education system to break the cycle of oppression and poverty. It is necessary to implement more funding for resources—high-quality tutoring, teachers, counselors, more engaging software, devices, and internet—as well as a more diverse teacher workforce, teacher training on implicit bias, true racial integration, and a culturally responsive and social justice curriculum that focuses on anti-Black racism and structural inequalities. When we prioritize Black children and anti-Black racism policy, we will build an education system and a nation committed to erasing education gaps. This change is the ultimate call for social justice and to give all children the opportunity to reach their full potential in the United States.

Works Cited

Bueno, Carycruz. "Bricks and Mortar vs. Computers and Modems: The Impacts of Enrollment in K-12 Virtual Schools." EdWorking-Paper, 20–250, Annenberg Institute, Brown University, Providence, RI, 2020. https://doi.org/10.26300/kahb-5v62.

Coleman, James. *Equality of Educational Opportunity.* Washington, D.C.: National Center for Educational Statistics, 1966.

Conrad, Cecilia A., John Whitehead, Patrick L. Mason, and James Stewart. *African Americans in the U.S. Economy.* Lanham, MD: Rowman & Littlefield, 2005.

Francis, Dania V. "Sugar and Spice and Everything Nice? Teacher Perceptions of Black Girls in the Classroom." *Review of Black Political Economy* 39 (2012): 311–320.

Jackson, C. Kirabo, Rucker C. Johnson, and Claudia Persico. "Boosting Educational Attainment and Adult Earnings." *Education Next* 15, no. 4 (2015): 69–76. https://www.educationnext.org/boosting-education-attainment-adult-earnings-school-spending/.

Johnson, Rucker, and Alexander Nazarian. *Children of the Dream: Why School Integration Works.* New York: Basic Books, 2019.

Lindsay, Constance A., and Cassandra M. D. Hart. "Teacher Race and School Discipline." *Education Next* 17, no. 1 (2017). https://www.educationnext.org/teacher-race-and-school-discipline-suspensions-research/.

$23 Billion. Jersey City, NJ: EdBuild, 2019. https://edbuild.org/content/23-billion/full-report.pdf.

ON THE BRILLIANCE OF BLACK GIRLS: TEACHING AND NURTURING IN SCHOOLS ACROSS AMERICA

Lauren Mims

Imagine yourself in a high school classroom immediately after school. It is the instructor's, a Black woman in her early twenties, first day launching a new culturally grounded after-school program designed to support Black girls' identity development and academic achievement. She has a homemade sheet cake with girl astronauts walking on the moon, polka-dot paper plates, rainbow-colored balls of yarn, piles of colored sheets of paper, and buckets of markers laid out in front of her. She begins to address the twenty girls in the classroom, who are quietly mumbling about why they were asked to stay after school. "Welcome to our very first session," the instructor says with a huge smile. Some girls whisper hello, while others glance at the clock.

"So, why do you think you were recommended for this program?" the instructor asks. The instructor twirls the piece of chalk while she waits. "Uh . . . because I am a bad student!" one girl exclaims from the back of the room. Some girls nod in response, and the instructor pauses, wondering if she should write that response on the board. Her shoulders sag a bit, but she writes the phrase on the board as another student yells, "Because I am loud and ghetto!" followed by, "And because I am a teen mom!" Students continue listing all the negative reasons they must have been asked to stay after school for a new program.

Time feels like it stops as the girls continue to vocalize all the damaging beliefs they've absorbed about themselves. The instructor silently writes them all on the board. When everyone has a chance to share their thoughts, the instructor takes a different-colored piece of chalk and crosses out each damaging belief, beginning with "Because I am a bad student," which is replaced with "Because you have hopes and dreams." The instructor continues. "Because I am loud and ghetto" is replaced with "Because you have important perspectives and opinions." The instructor uses a caret to add the word *wonderful* before *teen mom*. She continues writing on the board silently while every girl watches her replace each damaging belief with a positive affirmation.

When the instructor finishes, she puts the chalk down, hides her shaking hands behind her back, and faces the girls in silence. "So, is it kinda like those special programs other kids get to go to?" a student asks. The instructor smiles and nods vigorously as the other girls excitedly begin to shout out new answers such as "To get better grades," "To apply to college," "To make my relationships better," "To be happy."

On that memorable first day of mine—I was indeed the instructor—I thought the girls would shout out positive reasons for why they thought they had been recommended. Instead, I found myself choking back tears in front of a chalkboard covered in damaging beliefs brought upon these Black girls by their educators. The messages the girls shouted when I first began writing on the board echo pervasive stereotypes held about Black girls by society—that Black children are "troublemakers" or "achieving at significantly lower rates than their white peers," as shown by my own empirical research.

These damaging perceptions and the resulting actions of teachers when interacting with Black girls are harmful and can negatively affect their learning, development, and overall well-being. For instance, when a Black girl asks a challenging question in class, she is often perceived as abrasive and aggressive, rather than assertive and outspoken. Additionally, school districts across the nation have dress code policies rooted in race, gender, and class stereotypes that reinforce the marginalization and oppression of Black girls (e.g., policies that punish traditionally Black hairstyles and head coverings). In turn, Black girls are more likely to be pushed out of classrooms and schools rather than nominated for gifted services, as evidenced by the overrepresentation of Black girls in school discipline and the underrepresentation of Black girls in gifted and talented education.

As award-winning author Jacqueline Woodson wrote *Another Brooklyn,* a story about Black girlhood, she asked herself, "What am I going to do about a time of my life in which the brilliance of Black girls had no mirror?" I ask: What are we going to do about a time in which the brilliance of Black girls is not mirrored in educational practices, policies, and research? We should be able to enter every classroom in America, pick up a piece of chalk, and listen to Black girls detail how schools and other educational environments have taught and nurtured them.

To reach that point, we must develop practices, policies, and research that reflect the brilliance of Black girls. We must work with and for the leagues of Black girls in schools across the nation to identify the most pressing challenges they experience in school and in life, as well as pinpoint what supports exist or must be created. In listening to Black girls for decades, I know that they are changemakers in their own right. We must take a seat at their tables, rather than merely offer a seat or two to select girls. Then we must act on what we hear to reimagine education with the brilliance of Black girls as axiomatic.

When Black girls relate experiences of being pushed out, we must work to refute and dismantle harsh and destructive disciplinary policies by passing school discipline legislation that explicitly limits and eventually eliminates the use of suspensions and expulsions, expands access to mental health services, and ensures that Black girls have access to a high-quality education every single academic year. When Black girls describe incidents of (mis)education, we must demand that educators and administrators are held accountable and that "dreamkeepers," successful teachers of African American students, receive funding, recognition, and support to develop and/or strengthen programming and practices that mirror the brilliance of Black girls.

The powerful, pervasive, and insidious stereotypes and ensuing actions by other educators in my students' lives primed them to assume our program was yet another form of punishment, rather than a celebration and invitation to join a league of extraordinary Black girls. It is a poignant illustration of how too many Black girls strive to learn and achieve in unsupportive contexts. Moving forward, every Black girl should be enrolled in a school that meets and exceeds their academic and psychological needs, interests, and skills. And every Black girl should walk into school and classroom spaces and learn as well as be safe, affirmed, recognized, and supported by their educators.

Works Cited

Civil Rights Data Collection. 2016.

DRESS CODED: Black Girls, Bodies, and Bias in D.C. Schools. Washington, D.C.: National Women's Law Center, 2018. https://nwlc.org/resources/dresscoded/.

Mims, L. C., and J. L. Williams. "'They Told Me What I Was Before I Could Tell Them What I Was': Black Girls' Ethnic-Racial Identity Development Within Multiple Worlds." *Journal of Adolescent Research* 35, no. 6 (2020): 754–779. https://doi.org/10.1177/0743558420913483.

Morris, E. W. "'Ladies' or 'Loudies'? Perceptions and Experiences of Black Girls in Classrooms." *Youth & Society* 38, no. 4 (2007): 490–515.

Morris, M. *Pushout: The Criminalization of Black Girls in Schools.* New York: New Press, 2016.

Young, E. Y. "The Four Personae of Racism: Educators' (Mis)understanding of Individual vs. Systemic Racism." *Urban Education* 46, no. 6 (2011): 1433–1460.

THE IMMEASURABLE VALUE OF
BLACK CHILDREN'S BOOKS

S. Mia Obiwo and Francheska Starks

Books, as tools for empowerment, can strengthen the self-awareness and confidence of children coping with the reality of racism while cultivating their cultural consciousness and critical-thinking abilities. As issues of racial injustice continue to affect Black people's lives disproportionately, it is crucial that Black children recognize their value and genius. Children's books can be used as cultural artifacts that present models through which readers can come to understand themselves and the world in which they live. Black children's books offer young readers the chance to examine the past, question the present, and ponder future actions through affirming stories of exhilaration and triumph.

The books that children and caregivers choose are extremely important, as those stories can affect how children view the world and their place in it. Young readers need to see themselves portrayed in picture books in authentic and accurate ways. Books, like mirrors, help reflect what children know and understand about themselves, including their racial and cultural backgrounds. Books can also serve as windows that offer children views beyond their personal experiences, which give them the opportunity to learn about cultural backgrounds that differ from their own. Children's books help youth make meaning as they come to recognize their common humanity and value cultural differences.

Children's ideas about their own race and others' races are formed in early childhood, regardless of whether the topic of race is directly addressed or completely ignored in their homes or schools. In the absence of intentional discussion of race, children may not develop the necessary skills to navigate and resist racism and other types of oppression. Books centering Black people allow African American children to gain a vehicle through which they can participate more fully in their textual and, thus, public presentation. Centering perspectives of Black people and their cultures is undoubtedly valuable for Black people and all people, specifically those who are similarly marginalized. Highlighting Black identities and histories defies dominant narratives of a single story and sets a precedent that values multiple perspectives and voices on historical and current events and experiences. If the goal is indeed a pluralistic America in which diversity of all kinds is embraced, positive and accurate views of Blackness and Black identities must be a priority.

African American children deserve to experience the self-love that comes from recognizing oneself in a book. Black children's literature evokes a process that (re)affirms the identities of African American youth by fostering an understanding that their lives and the lives of people like them are worthy of being told, considered, discussed, and celebrated. Ultimately, when we know the stories of our people and our culture, we begin to understand ourselves as humans.

The value of Black children's literature is that it holds the power to encourage and influence *all* children to think and act in ways that value individual and cultural identities and to respect differences among people. Non-minoritized communities also benefit from gaining access to the contours of Black life through books that center Black children. Furthermore, Black children's literature can also be used as an informative vehicle for strengthening the cultural competence and critical consciousness of all children. With a primary goal of making visible and representing Black experiences, culturally conscious books are essential. There is also the potential to cultivate criticality in children and adults by addressing important social issues such as voter's rights (*Granddaddy's Turn: A Journey to the Ballot Box* by Michael S. Bandy and Eric Stein) and racism (*Antiracist Baby* by Ibram X. Kendi). Kendi's book is an especially salient example with its timely and forward message of anti-racism, which serves as a call to action for children and their caregivers to acknowledge and confront racist ideologies and behaviors.

A wide range of factors contributes to the purposeful selection of quality Black children's texts, including the presence of diverse characters and perspectives, diversity of authorship, messaging about difference and inclusion, and other important characteristics of the text. Turning attention toward how texts reflect the past experiences, present struggles and triumphs, and the hopeful futures maintained by people of African descent is one way to narrow the scope of the search for quality Black children's literature. Black children's literature can also aid young readers with establishing beliefs as well as a set of literacy, social, and cultural practices that go beyond the typical scope of reading engagement and achievement.

The following questions position consumers of Black children's literature, both children and adults, to evaluate the quality of texts that center the experiences of Black people and their communities: How does the author position/describe Black families? Are Black families identified as a resource for thriving and survival? Is there a focus on perseverance and the pursuit of liberty and equality for people of African descent or only struggle? Does the book reflect multiple aspects of cultures (e.g., language, tradition, spirituality, religion, etc.) of people of African descent? By positioning themselves as critical consumers of Black children's literature, caregivers and teachers, people of color, and white people can contribute to fostering social equity and cultures of inclusion and diversity by foregrounding the perspectives of Black communities.

Some examples of text that may appeal to the critical book consumer's concern for intentional and authentic representations of Black characters and Black life include *The Undefeated,* written by Kwame Alexander and illustrated by Kadir Nelson, *The Stars and the Blackness Between Them* by Junauda Petrus, and *Hair Love* by Matthew Cherry. *The Undefeated* highlights examples of historical and present Black excellence, such as the election of former president Barack Obama, and demonstrates reverence for past accomplishments, admiration for the present, and hope for the futures of Black people. *The Stars and the Blackness Between Them* and *Hair Love* focus on the functions of Black family life by both demonstrating the complexities of the roles of immediate and extended relationships in child-rearing and adolescents' maturation and highlighting its role in resiliency and strength for its individual members.

Black children's literature matters for all children. Black stories demand recognition of the rich historical knowledge and diverse expressions of Black individuals and communities. Black children's literature reflects the world in which we live by centering the histories of Black people and providing commentary on the current state of social affairs. Importantly, Black stories also inspire hope. They demonstrate what is possible and what could be. The optimism Black stories elicit may be one of its most important functions—a conduit for showing all people, regardless of race, color, religion, sexuality, and so on, what may be possible if we use our imaginations to materialize a more equitable world.

Works Cited

Bishop, R. S. "Mirrors, Windows, and Sliding Glass Doors." *Perspectives* 6 (1990): ix–xi.

Derman-Sparks, L. "Empowering Children to Create a Caring Culture in a World of Differences." *Childhood Education* 70, no. 2 (1993): 66–71.

Kortenhaus, C., and J. Demarest. "Gender Role Stereotyping in Children's Literature: An Update." *Sex Roles* 28, no. 3–4 (1993): 219–232.

THE FUTURE OF WORK BEGINS WITH HISTORICALLY BLACK COLLEGES AND UNIVERSITIES

Kristen E. Broady

Since the founding of the first Historically Black College or University (HBCU) in 1837, HBCUs have persevered in their principal mission to educate African Americans. HBCUs are known for their rich history and rigorous academic programs despite a confluence of lower-than-average admission requirements, funding opportunities, limited technological resources, lower endowments, and smaller operating budgets on average as compared to predominantly white institutions (PWIs). They now face a new challenge: continuing to uphold the mission in the age of automation, which has been accelerated by the COVID-19 pandemic.

Even with technological advancements, including platforms such as Zoom, Google Hangouts, and learning management systems (LMS) such as Blackboard and Canvas, technology demands pose an additional burden for HBCU administrators, faculty, and students. Considering the limited capacity of Information Technology (IT) departments at smaller, lesser-resourced HBCUs, and the major investment necessary to maintain an online LMS, many HBCUs and minority-serving institutions struggled with the move to the virtual classroom at the beginning of the COVID-19 pandemic. An average of 75.4 percent of full-time first-time undergraduates at HB-CUs were awarded Pell grants—usually given to undergraduates with a high degree of unmet financial need—compared to 43.2 percent at PWIs, leading to concerns about students' ability to afford internet and laptop access at home. This disparity indicates that students who require the most support are more likely to be further disadvantaged by the move to virtual learning. The pandemic laid bare the need for increased investments in technological platforms, devices, and training for HBCU students and faculty.

Prior to the COVID-19 crisis, the nation and the world had already begun to wade into the Fourth Industrial Revolution, characterized by automation—artificial intelligence, the internet of things, mobile supercomputing, and intelligent robots. The COVID-19 pandemic is expected to accelerate automation in the U.S. According to a report by Forrester, many companies plan to invest more in automation technology than in rehiring workers because of the pandemic, thereby accelerating planned automation strategies that were in place prior to the pandemic. While there exists the assumption that technological investment may decrease during recessions, like the one caused by the pandemic, investment in automation is more likely to occur during economic downturns when human workers become relatively more expensive as firms' revenues rapidly decline. The acceleration of automation will have a disparate impact on Americans based on their race, occupation, and educational attainment, and even more of a negative impact on workers who are unable to work remotely.

About 25 percent of people employed in August 2020 had teleworked or worked from home for pay within the previous four weeks because of the COVID-19 pandemic—down from 35 percent in May 2020. Though, at the time, less than 5 percent of all occupations had the capability of being automated entirely using demonstrated technologies, about 60 percent of all occupations had at least 30 percent of constituent activities that could be automated, suggesting that more occupations will change than will be automated away. Education and workforce development will thus be necessary to combat the substantial skills gap that already exists in the American labor force and that will be exacerbated by the acceleration of automation.

In 2019, the top ten jobs most at risk to be automated, based on the automation risk scale created by Frey and Osborne (2013), employed the highest share of workers in the U.S.— amounting to nearly twenty-two million workers. Black workers are overrepresented in five of these jobs: cashiers; laborers and freight, stock, and material movers and handlers; cooks; office clerks; and receptionists and information clerks. Many of these jobs were also considered essential, meaning that workers in these jobs continued to work in-person when many businesses closed due to social distancing orders, increasing their risk of contracting COVID-19.

The need to equip students with a functional understanding of technology, theory, and soft skills can be a challenge for most educational institutions, but the challenge is magnified for HBCUs due to revenue constraints via lower average tuition and endowment funds. Therefore, funding for technical infrastructure, training for students and faculty, and information technology (IT) department staffing at HBCUs are critical to mitigating trends in disparities in access to employment in occupations that are at lower risk of being automated.

Considering the overrepresentation of Black workers in

occupations at high risk of being automated, the mission of HBCUs must be realigned to prepare Black college students for the future of work with automation. A new model of education should be introduced to blend technical and social training to prepare students to move between various jobs and tasks. While faculty members have been prepared to teach various quantitative and qualitative courses in their specific fields of study, they must also be prepared to embed lessons on conflict negotiation and resolution, verbal and written communication, content creation, empathy, planning, and leadership into their courses, while also teaching students how to fully utilize relevant data-analytic tools and programs.

Through existing and new networks between HBCUs, PWIs, and corporations, cooperative education programs should be developed to share accumulated knowledge, provide efficient pipelines from undergraduate to graduate programs, and collaboratively communicate with corporations and business leaders regarding requirements for internships and employment opportunities for graduates. HBCUs should also conduct periodic program reviews to assess the automation readiness of their majors and program offerings to determine if they are preparing students for jobs that will exist or for jobs that will be drastically altered or eliminated due to automation.

With funding from organizations like the United Negro College Fund (UNCF), HBCUs are creating innovative programs and partnerships to prepare students to face the future of work. The UNCF Career Pathways Initiative (CPI), funded by the Lilly Endowment, is a $50 million investment over a seven-year period that helps four-year HBCUs and predominantly Black institutions strengthen institutional career placement outcomes to increase the number of graduates who are prepared to immediately transition to meaningful jobs in their respective fields. Dillard University, in New Orleans, Louisiana, is the recipient of a UNCF CPI Liberal Arts Innovation Center (LAIC) grant and used the funds to create the Center for Automation Readiness and Employment (CARE). Talladega College is using UNCF CPI LAIC grant funds to institute an interactive professional learning process for faculty, which will lead to increased student learning and retention. Professors will study student responses to active learning strategies during technology-enhanced lessons using a variety of techniques to include training models focusing on critical-thinking, communication, and problem-solving skills.

The continued injection of automation into the American economy will increase economic growth, output, and efficiency. If Black students are to be prepared to enter the post-COVID economy, HBCUs must play a vital role in their training and development.

Works Cited

Aoun, J. E. *Robot-Proof: Higher Education in the Age of Artificial Intelligence.* Cambridge: MIT Press, 2018.

Broady, K. E., Todd, C. L., and Booth-Bell, D. Dreaming and Doing at Georgia HBCUs: Continued Relevancy in 'Post-Racial' America. *The Review of Black Political Economy,* 44(1–2), 37–54.

Bureau of Labor Statistics, U.S. Department of Labor, The Economics Daily, One-quarter of the employed teleworked in August 2020 because of COVID-19 pandemic at https://www.bls.gov/opub/ted/2020/one-quarter-of-the-employed-teleworked-in-august-2020-because-of-covid-19-pandemic.htm.

Chandler, S. Chander, Simon. "Coronavirus Is Forcing Companies to Speed Up Automation, for Better and for Worse." *Forbes.* May 12, 2020. https://www.forbes.com/sites/simonchandler/2020/05/12/ corona-virus-is-forcingcompanies-to-speed-up-automation-forbetter-and-for-worse/#2e72eb7a5906.

Frey, Carl Benedikt, and Osborne, Michael A. "The Future of Employment: How Susceptible Are Jobs to Computerisation?" *Technological Forecasting and Social Change* 114 (2013): 254–280.

Manyika, J., Chui, M., and Miremadi, M. "A future That Works: AI, Automation, Employment, and Productivity." Manyika, J., Chui, M., Miremadi, M., Bughin, J., George, K, and Willmott, P., et. al. McKinsey Global Institute Research, Tech. Rep 60, 1–135.

Muro, M., Maxim, R., and Whiton, J. The robots are ready as the COVID-19 recession spreads. The Brookings Institution. March 24, 2020.

U.S. Department of Education, National Center for Education Statistics. The Condition of Education 2021 (NCES Report No. 2021-144). Washington, DC: U.S. Government Printing Office; 2021.

Schwab, K. *The Fourth Industrial Revolution.* New York: Crown Business. 2017.

THE CASE FOR (BLACK) STUDENT LOAN DEBT FORGIVENESS

Fenaba R. Addo

When we hear the statistic that 35 percent of Americans hold a college degree, it masks that there are a considerably greater number of individuals who have some postsecondary experience but no degree, and an increasingly substantial number of people with student debt and no degree. More adults are going to college and taking on loans to do so, a growing portion of which are Black students, whose share of undergraduate representation increased from 12.3 percent to 15.2 percent between 1995/96 and 2015/16. Despite federal financial aid becoming more generous, state and institutional aid per student have declined over time, shifting these costs to students and their families, who have turned to debt to make up the difference between family resources and rising costs.

At all levels of higher education, Black students are more likely to borrow for their degrees. They also take on more debt for their degrees. For example, Black students composed 12 percent of all bachelor's degree recipients in 2015/2016; 64 percent, or almost two-thirds, have over $30,000 in debt, and a third have over $40,000. Default rates, defined as a missed payment for 270 days on federal loans, for student debt, also differ by race. Default rates for Black borrowers exceed white borrowers independent of whether or not they completed their studies. And ten years postgraduation, Black borrowers owed 51 percent of their initial loan debt, and 21 percent had some experience with nonpayment either through loan deferment or forbearance.

Racial disparities in debt are large and increase throughout early adult life. Due to racial wealth inequalities, Black parents have fewer economic resources to protect young adult children from high debt burdens. Racial differences in initial loan debt are significant; Black young adults hold 55 percent more debt than their white counterparts after accounting for family background and young adult characteristics. Moreover, the Black-white student loan debt disparity increases over the course of young adulthood, growing by about 7.2 percent annually. In other words, Black youth start their young adult careers with more debt than white people, and this gap grows over time. What is even more alarming is that Black people are paying down their debt at a rate of 2.09 percent compared with a 9.5 percent rate for white young adults. Inequalities in postsecondary institutional and credit market characteristics, along with the labor markets and life circumstances these young adults experience upon leaving school, lead Black people to repay their loans more slowly than their white peers.

One place to begin understanding the disparity is by looking at institution type. Black adults are more likely to enroll in for-profit institutions or attend underfunded schools, which are associated with higher levels of debt accumulation. According to Pew Research Center, in 2015, about 9 percent of Black students enrolled at HBCU institutions (approximately 300,000 students across 101 institutions), and they graduated about 15 percent of all bachelor's degrees earned by Black students. A 2016 report from the United Negro College Fund showed that the largest endowment for an HBCU (Howard University, $600 million) is significantly lower than the endowment of the tenth-place non-HBCU university (University of Michigan, $9.5 billion). More students who attend an HBCU have federal loans and on average have more debt; specifically, Black parents of children who attended HBCUs have some of the largest Parent PLUS loans.

Undeniably, these racial disparities in student debt are contributing to Black-white wealth inequality among a recent cohort of college-going young adults. In our own research, we found that if Black youth had the same debt burden as white youth, the racial wealth gap would decrease by approximately 10.5 percent. The implications for these differences have both immediate and longer-term consequences. Since white adults borrow less for college and repay their outstanding loan amounts faster, they can begin to save and build their wealth while Black young adults are still repaying their loans. These patterns reflect trends in wage discrimination and higher unemployment as well as hark back to historical legacies of structural inequalities created as a result of racist public policies that denied wealth accumulation pathways for Black Americans. Racial wealth inequality persists intergenerationally; it contributes to present-day differences in debt accumulation that add to racial gaps in wealth within this young adult population.

Much of the current discourse to address the student debt crisis focuses on piecemeal solutions or market-based solutions that may continue to perpetuate a debt-financed system that burdens marginalized populations. For example, recent calls to focus only on income-driven repayment (IDR) plans either ignore the racialized nature of the student debt and repayment crisis or deliberately disregard the plight of the most vulnerable. These solutions say because you and your family lacked the resources to afford your college education and may be more likely to receive lower pay and lower wage growth or experience unemployment, you will ultimately pay more for that education. Steinbaum (2020) shows that repayment plans are not addressing the economic resource constraints of current borrowers, disproportionately Black borrowers. According to the College Board, almost a third of direct loan borrowers were in IDRs, which consists of income-based repayment (IBR), income-contingent repayment (ICR), Pay as You Earn (PAYE) and, the newest offering, Revised Pay as You Earn (REPAYE) plans. These plans differ in the amount required to repay (e.g., 5 percent, 10 percent, 15 percent of discretionary income), length of repayment period, who qualifies based on loan-type eligibility, or debt to income. Recent analysis indicates that the median Black borrower still owed 95 percent of the original balance of their student debt after twenty years in repayment.

Returning to the example of HBCU students, in May 2019, Robert Smith, an African American billionaire, announced during his commencement speech at Morehouse College a pledge to eliminate the student loan debt of the graduating class, an estimated $34 million, following that with a pledge to include parental debt. A year later in 2020, millionaire Frank Baker donated $1 million to pay the student loan debt of fifty graduating seniors at Spelman College. While these acts are undoubtedly transformative for the students who received debt relief, reliance on philanthropic gifts to solve a policy failure raises thorny questions. For example, the financial burden of graduates who were lucky enough to receive this gift is undoubtedly lighter, but what about subsequent classes? And what about students who graduated from less elite institutions

with no millionaire or billionaire alumni? To date, we have decided that students and their families should bear a significant
portion of the costs despite evidence that the added value of a
postsecondary degree accrues beyond the individual. Relying
on the donations of private wealthy alumni may only serve
to perpetuate existing societal inequalities, especially if only a
small number of targeted borrowers receive assistance.

There has also been a growing interest and investment in
income contingent financing programs such as income share
agreements (ISAs). These are investment products primarily
funded by venture capital firms that offer students low-interest
loans to cover their tuition while enrolled. In exchange, students
then pay a portion of the income for a specified period of
time, post-degree, back to the ISA provider. ISA advocates
believe these should be an attractive alternative financing
product because contracted students only pay a percentage
rather than fixed amount of their earnings; there is no principal
balance or interest. At the end of the contracted term, students
are no longer obligated to pay any additional monies. There is
very little information on ISAs and similar programs and their
effectiveness, yet they are receiving lots of attention and financial support from Wall Street and beyond. It is important to
be cautious, however. Dr. Rhonda Vonshay Sharpe points out
that Black graduates not only earn less but are concentrated
in majors that have lower average earnings. As a result, this
innovation may not be equitable as Black (and low-income)
students would be disproportionately burdened by such an
arrangement. Some ISAs may have thresholds for individuals
who earn below a certain income, but similar to IDR plans,
they will need to pay once their income increases.

The student debt and repayment crisis for Black borrowers

requires a two-pronged approach. The first prong calls for debt cancellation for all borrowers holding loan debt associated with their college years to address the outstanding debt burden. There should be no cap for debt cancellation, given Black borrowers carry more debt on average with balances growing over time. Concluding that debt cancellation is wrong because some financially better-off borrowers will receive a greater benefit than others is a weak argument. It centers a small percentage of upper-income, high-balance borrowers at the expense of the larger population of Black borrowers and low-balance, lower-income borrowers. Why not give debt relief that many of us who had debt or repaid their debts would have wanted, and work to build a better system?

The second prong must address student debt accumulation. There were many proposals during the 2020 presidential election to address the student debt crisis. While most tackled the repayment crisis, a few contained prescriptions to address the accumulation phase, focusing on tuition and higher education costs. For example, President Joseph Biden's plan proposed two years of free community college based on a federal-state partnership. Senator Elizabeth Warren's plan was the only one to include increased funding to HBCU, tribal, and other minority-serving institutions. None of these proposals, however, address the central problem—the lack of resources within Black households. And, in fact, as Darity, Addo, and Smith (2020) show, many anti-poverty policy proposals will do little to close existing wealth gaps. To really address the debt accumulation crisis, there needs to be a greater focus on increasing the wealth of Black households.

As part of the CARES Act, in response to the COVID-19 crisis, payments on federal student debt were postponed interest-free through September 30, and then subsequently extended through December 31 (by executive action). That the U.S. government prioritized student loan debt acknowledges both the potential adverse effects that debt can have on households facing all these issues as well as the awareness of this burden in the lives of many Americans. COVID-19 and the CARES Act showed us that temporary student debt relief is possible. Now is the time to make it permanent and refocus efforts on financial security and wealth-building for Black students and their families.

Works Cited

Addo, Fenaba R., Jason N. Houle, and Daniel Simon. "Young, Black, and (Still) in the Red: Parental Wealth, Race, and Student Loan Debt." *Race and Social Problems* 8, no. 1 (2016): 64–76. https://doi.org/10.1007/s12552-016-9162-0.

Anderson, Monica. "A Look at Historically Black Colleges and Universities as Howard Turns 150." *Pew Research Center* (blog), February 28, 2017. https://www.pewresearch.org/fact-tank/2017 /02/28/a-look-at-historically-black-colleges-and-universities-as -howard-turns-150/.

Espinosa, Lorelle L., Jonathan M. Turk, Morgan Taylor, and Hollie M. Chessman. *Race and Ethnicity in Higher Education: A Status Report*. Washington, D.C.: American Council on Education, 2019.

Houle, Jason N., and Fenaba R. Addo. "Racial Disparities in Student Debt and the Reproduction of the Fragile Black Middle Class." *Sociology of Race and Ethnicity* 5, no. 4 (2019): 562–577.

Lochner, Lance J., and Alexander Monge-Naranjo. "Default and Repayment Among Baccalaureate Degree Earners." National Bureau of Economic Research working paper, February 2014. https://www.nber.org/papers/w19882.

Looney, Adam, and Constantine Yannelis. "A Crisis in Student Loans? How Changes in the Characteristics of Borrowers and in the Institutions They Attended Contributed to Rising Loan Defaults." Brookings Papers on Economic Activity, fall 2015. http://www.brookings.edu/about/projects/bpea/papers/2015 /looney-yannelis-student-loan-defaults.

Ma, Jennifer, Matea Pender, and Meredith Welch. *Education Pays*

2016: The Benefits of Higher Education for Individuals and Society.
New York: College Board, 2016.

Mitchell, Josh, and Andrea Fuller. "The Student-Debt Crisis Hits
Hardest at Historically Black Colleges." *Wall Street Journal,* April
17, 2019. https://www.wsj.com/articles/the-student-debt-crisis
-hits-hardest-at-historically-black-colleges-11555511327.

"Opinion: Forgiving Student Loans the Wrong Way Will Only
Worsen Inequality." *Washington Post,* December 3, 2020.
https://www.washingtonpost.com/opinions/forgiving-student
-loans-the-wrong-way-will-only-worsen-inequality/2020/12/03
/2650d384–34c9–11eb-8d38–6aea1adb3839_story.html.

Reilly, Katie. "Robert F. Smith Launches New HBCU Student Debt
Initiative." *Time,* June 23, 2020. https://time.com/5857186
/robert-f-smith-historically-black-colleges/.

Saunders, Katherine M., Krystal L. Williams, and Cheryl L. Smith.
*Fewer Resources, More Debt: Loan Debt Burdens Students at
Historically Black Colleges and Universities.* Washington, D.C.:
UNCF, 2016.

Scott-Clayton, Judith. "The Looming Student Loan Default Crisis Is
Worse Than We Thought." Brookings, January 11, 2018. https://
www.brookings.edu/research/the-looming-student-loan-default
-crisis-is-worse-than-we-thought/.

Sharpe, Rhonda Vonshay. "ISAs-Income Share Agreements Are
Debt: Maybe Even Predatory." Women's Institute for Science,
Equity and Race. https://www.wiserpolicy.org/isas/.

Steinbaum, Marshall. "The Student Debt Crisis Is a Crisis of Non-
Repayment." Phenomenal World, November 11, 2020. https://
phenomenalworld.org/analysis/crisis-of-non-repayment.

Sullivan, Laura, Tatjana Meschede, Thomas Shapiro, and Fernanda
Escobar. *Stalling Dreams: How Student Debt Is Disrupting Life*

Chances and Widening the Racial Wealth Gap. Waltham, MA: Institute for Assets and Social Policy, 2019.

Trends in College Pricing and Student Aid 2020. New York: College Board, 2020.

"Who Is Robert F. Smith, the Billionaire behind the Morehouse Graduation Gift?" *USA Today,* May 20, 2019. https://www .usatoday.com/story/money/2019/05/20/robert-f-smith-who -billionaire-behind-morehouse-graduation-gift/3739290002/.

PART V

TECHNOLOGY

The digital space and its global tentacles manifest bigotry in new and different ways that previous generations haven't experienced.

—DR. BRANDEIS MARSHALL

In late 2020, Timnit Gebru, a prominent artificial intelligence (AI) researcher, was ousted by Google after expressing frustration with the lack of transparency over a research paper retraction. Less than a year later, her colead was fired as well. The backlash was swift and led many to question the role Black people played within the technology industry despite ongoing efforts to diversify and include historically marginalized voices. As time would show, those willing to speak out about how the technology industry should engage with the Black community were primarily Black women—a demographic that, by the most recent numbers, represents less than half of 1 percent of Silicon Valley's technology workforce, according to Arizona State University and Pivotal Ventures. Yet Black women have, and continue to be, the pioneers of groundbreaking research regarding facial recognition bias with little to no credit in the mainstream. Black women, as it turns out, are the anchors of the future of technology.

The Black [TECHNOLOGY] Agenda discusses how systems such as AI and facial recognition not only embed biases in how they are created but also inherently mimic those biases in who is credited as an expert within those spaces. The experts included in this chapter are all computer science researchers.

Each, in their own unique way, points out the importance of ethical standards that can prevent the perpetuation of discrimination by existing and forthcoming technology as well as the need for precise language to describe the unethical practices taking place currently. In this chapter, readers will hear from:

- **Deborah Raji,** an award-winning computer scientist, known for her joint work with Joy Buolamwini regarding Amazon's facial recognition bias, who recounts her experience with "Big Tech" and erasure while pointing to policy-oriented solutions that push for accountability in technology spaces.

- Professor **Brandeis Marshall,** who advises Black people to use "digital smarts" to fight against algorithmic assault, which she defines as codified attacks on Black bodies through digital mechanisms. Marshall emphasizes the importance of language with respect to how technology is being used to undermine Black lives in the new digital age.

- Machine learning expert and content creator **Jordan Harrod,** who pushes against the current definition of artificial intelligence while emphasizing the need for specific language and standards to properly address the harms being committed against marginalized groups in the name of technological advancement.

FACING THE TECH GIANTS

Deborah Raji

On January 26, 2019, the then general manager of artificial intelligence at Amazon Web Services (AWS), published a short blog post. It was an exceptionally quick response, released just days after my coauthor, Joy Buolamwini, and I published a peer-reviewed audit study. Our study assessed the quality of an increasingly popular Amazon Artificial Intelligence (AI) product used to analyze and identify face images. Our results revealed that, for minority populations, this product's performance fell short. When predicting the gender of individuals from their facial appearance, we found that the Amazon product was over 30 percent less effective on darker female faces than lighter male faces.

Amazon's reply to this audit outcome characterized the research as "false and misleading," claiming that we failed to "put the accuracy in context." Amazon's critique mentioned multiple times that their team had "not been able to reproduce the results of the study" using the most recent version of the product, which involved "a significant set of improvements in November." However, upon closer scrutiny, Amazon's narrative was unpersuasive. The blog post explicitly mentioned that the audit was conducted on August 21, 2018—months before the November "improvements," but using the exact same product version that Amazon was at the time attempting to pitch for use by police departments and U.S. Immigration and Customs Enforcement (ICE). Over time, Amazon's reproducibility claims crumbled as more and more companies, regulators, and researchers simply proved Amazon's claims wrong, reproducing the results and rallying in defense of our study.

Audits like the one my coauthor and I had carried out stand as a mechanism for accountability to reveal the limitations of a technology for the protection of those dealing with it. In that moment, and its aftermath, I realized that what Amazon had failed to see, quite literally, was me. Not only was their product failing for Black female faces like mine, but they were attempting to dismiss the concerns raised about their technology by Black female voices like mine.

There's a double cost to every algorithmic audit study we, as young Black women, conduct. One challenge is the issue of articulating with evidence the reality of a technological deployment that doesn't work for *us*. This means everything from demonstrating that an app labels photos of *our* Black faces as "gorillas" to vocalizing how social media moderation filters censor *our* essential phrases, like "Black Lives Matter." Conducting this kind of research means systematically proving how racial prejudice perpetuated by criminal risk assessments disproportionately flags Black defendants—members of our community—as high risk while simultaneously raising their bail and keeping them in jail. It also means testing AI tools used in everything from hiring to housing to health care that may be skewed against our favor. It is emotionally taxing work to relate harm tied to personal identity to a homogenous tech world that often hasn't previously been paying much attention and likely does not want to listen. Because this is the second issue—the unspoken postscript to every audit: the long battle to be heard.

My coauthors, also Black women, and I are constantly entreating others to take our work seriously—to listen to us, to properly cite our work, and to include us in pertinent discussion. We continue to do this even long after we have had our results verified and proven right many times over. Instead of dialogue or rapt attention, we are met with accusatory blog posts and dismissal. Instead of embracing our unique perspectives, the industry pushes us out.

The tragedy of the tech industry is not that we struggle to anticipate the built technology and its risks; it's that those that most clearly see the dangers can also be those most easily dismissed. I learned this several years ago when I was an anxious intern at a young computer vision start-up sifting through a catalog of faces that did not include me, to develop one of several AI models I suspected would not work for me. I recall enthusiastically presenting these concerns to my manager at the time and being met by a frigid indifference. Like many marginalized voices, I've always known what could go wrong, but often found myself being regularly doubted. The audacity of our critics at Amazon and those like them, dismissing the minorities rightfully raising concerns about the tech industry and its products, represents a fundamental resistance to those most intent on holding this industry accountable for the harm they contribute to.

This is why tech accountability policy needs to leave the door open for outsiders to participate. We cannot rely on companies to identify the right problems and listen to the right perspectives on their own. External auditors examine a system from the outside to evaluate its effectiveness and communicate evidence of concerns to the public. These are the auditors that best represent the interest of those impacted but will often lack direct access to that system, as they have no contractual relationship with the company itself (i.e., are not hired consultants or employees of the company). Their motive, instead, is the protection of those most impacted and most at risk of harm from technological deployments—those they feel compelled to represent.

To solicit and address a diverse range of concerns, external auditors need to be given access through regulators to the information they need from corporations to perform their audits. Furthermore, they need to be legally protected as they ask important questions and evaluate these products from the outside. When legally challenged by technology companies for making use of products or accessing product data for audit purposes, auditors have in the past been vulnerable to having their audit activities legally framed as a type of computer hacking, against which there are quite strict laws. If such audits are government mandated and facilitated—legally requiring corporate cooperation and a response—then it becomes that much more difficult for institutions to brush these outsiders aside.

The idea of allowing external perspectives to scrutinize deployed technology has crystallized over the years, materializing in concrete policy interventions. The Algorithmic Justice and Online Platform Transparency Act, California Algorithmic Accountability Bill, and Algorithmic Accountability Act of 2019 in the U.S. and the Digital Services Act (notably, Article 32 and Article 28) from the European Commission are all recent policy proposals with articles to actually mandate such audits and have government agencies, like the Federal Trade Commission, facilitate external participation in flagging and evaluating potentially discriminatory technology products.

Furthermore, the audit community is slowly maturing—

developing audit tools, resources, methodology, and training materials to facilitate the audit process for those coming into the field. As a result, an increasing diversity of individuals and institutions have begun to participate in the process—not just traditional academics but also investigative journalists from ProPublica or the Markup; regulators from agencies like the Federal Trade Commission (FTC), the National Institute of Standards and Technology (NIST), and the Government Accountability Office (GAO); advocacy organizations like the Algorithmic Justice League and Data for Black Lives; and legal firms like Foxglove. These organizations operate as outsiders committed to scrutinizing the systems that impact us, challenging tech companies and their performance claims in defense of the rights and liberties of communities that are often overlooked.

Grassroots algorithmic auditors are even leveraging relationships with more established advocacy organizations like the American Civil Liberties Union (ACLU), to feed audit results into lawsuits or public campaigns for accountability. In a landmark case (*Sandvig v. Barr*), the ACLU fought for the protection of researchers analyzing discriminatory technology outcomes against accusations under the Computer Fraud and Abuse Act (CFAA). In another case, the ACLU was able to sue Facebook into releasing the internal information required to audit the discriminatory outcomes of their ad delivery algorithm, providing a template to demand through civil suit settlements the required information from tech companies to conduct audits in the first place. Leveraging our own audit results on facial recognition products, the ACLU successfully campaigned for a plethora of bans and restrictions on the use of the technology throughout cities in the U.S.

Though they publicly attempted to discredit us, Amazon internally acknowledged the reality of the issues raised and took a set of private, unadvertised actions. Over time, they would flip-flop on the recommended and enforced product settings and invest millions to sponsor a National Science Foundation grant on fair performance as well as hire a fairness lead. The head of policy at Amazon parroted similar positions to past audit targets Microsoft and IBM, declaring the intent of the company to support facial recognition regulation in light of concerns, and, like Microsoft, they hired an army of lobbyists to dominate each facial recognition bill that entered Congress. Amazon would later attempt to block the shareholder vote on banning the company's sale of facial recognition, and when ordered by the U.S. Securities and Exchange Commission to allow for the vote, they aggressively campaigned shareholders to vote against the memo. At the end of the day, they refused to participate in the government-conducted audit of their facial recognition product while continuing to publicly deny and deflect these realities, as a particularly violent form of corporate gaslighting.

After two long years of exhausting advocacy—in the company of advocates at ACLU and Fight for the Future, and in the wave of racial anger prompted by George Floyd's murder—on June 10, 2020, Amazon finally budged. Finally, for at least this brief moment, the company was successfully pressured to remove a questionably functional and dangerous technology from the market. This was followed by an announcement to pause the sale of their facial recognition technology to police clients. The moratorium, which would later get extended to an indefinite voluntary recall, was the closest we saw to the company recognizing our demands. We celebrated, thinking we had won something.

But Robert Williams, a native of Michigan, wasn't celebrating. He was too busy preparing for an upcoming legal battle after experiencing the trauma of being handcuffed and dragged away by police in front of his daughter, following his false arrest due to a wrong facial recognition match. He was too occupied recovering from the confusion and fear of sitting in an interrogation room the day before his forty-second birthday because yet another product marketed to protect him instead made him vulnerable and put him in serious danger. Similarly, in February 2019, days after that Amazon blog post and in the midst of its fallout, Nijeer Parks was arrested, spending ten days in jail and over $5,000 to defend himself from a crime he didn't commit, all because of a false facial recognition match.

In an industry so insular and uniform that it misses or dismisses every outsider's concern, every win is too late—each intervention arriving years after the issue has been raised, allowing for even more unnecessary suffering. Our courage to flick our stones at tech giants comes from an awareness of what happens if we don't. In the absence of our wearied cries, there's nothing. Worse than being ignored are the consequences of silence. We are here for ourselves and the communities we love, and this provides enough strength to keep going—to hit our targets with precision, and watch as the giants fall.

Works Cited

"ACLU of Michigan Complaint Re Use of Facial Recognition." ACLU. https://www.aclu.org/letter/aclu-michigan-complaint-re-use-facial-recognition.

Angwin, Julia, Jeff Larson, Surya Mattu, and Lauren Kirchner. "Machine Bias." ProPublica, May 23, 2016. https://www.propublica.org/article/machine-bias-risk-assessments-in-criminal-sentencing.

Bass, Dina. "Amazon Schooled on AI Facial Technology by Turing Award Winner." Bloomberg, April 3, 2019. https://www.bloomberg.com/news/articles/2019–04–03/amazon-schooled-on-ai-facial-technology-by-turing-award-winner.

Boutin, Chad. "NIST Study Evaluates Effects of Race, Age, Sex on Face Recognition Software." NIST, December 19, 2019. https://www.nist.gov/news-events/news/2019/12/nist-study-evaluates-effects-race-age-sex-face-recognition-software.

"Community Control Over Police Surveillance (CCOPS) Model Bill." ACLU. Updated April 2021. https://www.aclu.org/legal-document/community-control-over-police-surveillance-ccops-model-bill.

Cook, C. M., J. J. Howard, Y. B. Sirotin, J. L. Tipton, and A. R. Vemury. "Demographic Effects in Facial Recognition and Their Dependence on Image Acquisition: An Evaluation of Eleven Commercial Systems." *IEEE Transactions on Biometrics, Behavior, and Identity Science* 1, no. 1 (2019): 32–41. https://ieeexplore.ieee.org/document/8636231. doi: 10.1109/TBIOM.2019.2897801.

Dastin, Jeffrey. "Amazon Scraps Secret AI Recruiting Tool

That Showed Bias Against Women." Reuters, October 10, 2018. https://www.reuters.com/article/us-amazon-com-jobs-automation-insight/amazon-scraps-secret-ai-recruiting-tool-that-showed-bias-against-women-idUSKCN1MK08G.

Guliani, Neema Singh. "Amazon Met with ICE Officials to Market Its Facial Recognition Product." ACLU, October 24, 2018. https://www.aclu.org/blog/privacy-technology/surveillance-technologies/amazon-met-ice-officials-market-its-facial.

Hao, Karen. "The Two-Year Fight to Stop Amazon from Selling Face Recognition to the Police." *MIT Technology Review*, June 12, 2020. https://www.technologyreview.com/2020/06/12/1003482/amazon-stopped-selling-police-face-recognition-fight/.

Hao, Karen. "We Read the Paper That Forced Timnit Gebru Out of Google. Here's What It Says." *MIT Technology Review*, December 4, 2020. https://www.technologyreview.com/2020/12/04/1013294/google-ai-ethics-research-paper-forced-out-timnit-gebru/.

Hill, Kashmir. "Another Arrest, and Jail Time, Due to a Bad Facial Recognition Match." *New York Times*, December 29, 2020. https://www.nytimes.com/2020/12/29/technology/facial-recognition-misidentify-jail.html.

Hill, Kashmir. "Wrongfully Accused by an Algorithm." *New York Times*, June 24, 2020. https://www.nytimes.com/2020/06/24/technology/facial-recognition-arrest.html.

"IBM Response to 'Gender Shades: Intersectional Accuracy Disparities in Commercial Gender Classification.'" Gender Shades. http://gendershades.org/docs/ibm.pdf.

Johnson, Carolyn Y. "Racial Bias in a Medical Algorithm Favors White Patients over Sicker Black Patients." *Washington Post*, October 24, 2019. https://www.washingtonpost.com/health

/2019/10/24/racial-bias-medical-algorithm-favors-white-patients
-over-sicker-black-patients/.

Kirchner, Lauren. "The Obscure Yet Powerful Tenant-Screening
Industry Is Finally Getting Some Scrutiny." Markup, January
11, 2021. https://themarkup.org/locked-out/2021/01/11/the
-obscure-yet-powerful-tenant-screening-industry-is-finally
-getting-some-scrutiny.

Laperruque, Jake. "About-Face: Examining Amazon's Shifting Story
on Facial Recognition Accuracy." POGO, April 10, 2019.
https://www.pogo.org/analysis/2019/04/about-face-examining
-amazon-shifting-story-on-facial-recognition-accuracy/.

McShane, Julianne. "'60 Minutes' Ran an Episode About Algorithm
Bias. Only White Experts Were Given Airtime." Lily, June 11,
2021. https://www.thelily.com/60-minutes-ran-an-episode-about
-algorithm-bias-only-white-experts-were-given-airtime/.

"NSF Program on Fairness in Artificial Intelligence in Collaboration
with Amazon (FAI)." National Science Foundation. https://www
.nsf.gov/funding/pgm_summ.jsp?pims_id=505651.

Raji, Inioluwa Deborah, and Joy Buolamwini. "Actionable Auditing:
Investigating the Impact of Publicly Naming Biased Performance Results of Commercial AI Products." *Proceedings of the
2019 AAAI/ACM Conference on AI, Ethics, and Society,* January
2019: 429–435. https://dl.acm.org/doi/abs/10.1145/3306618
.3314244.

Reuters Staff. "U.S. SEC Blocks Amazon Effort to Stop Shareholder Votes on Racial Equity Audit." Reuters. https://www
.reuters.com/article/us-amazon-com-sec-vote/u-s-sec-blocks
-amazon-effort-to-stop-shareholder-votes-on-racial-equity-audit
-idUSKBN2BU38U.

Roach, John. "Microsoft Improves Facial Recognition Technology
to Perform Well Across All Skin Tones, Genders." *AI Blog,* June

26, 2018. https://blogs.microsoft.com/ai/gender-skin-tone-facial
-recognition-improvement/.

Romano, Benjamin. "Amazon's Role in AI Fairness Research Raises
Eyebrows." *Government Technology,* April 1, 2019. https://www
.govtech.com/products/amazons-role-in-ai-fairness-research
-raises-eyebrows.html.

"Sandvig v. Barr—Challenge to CFAA Prohibition on Uncover-
ing Racial Discrimination Online." ACLU. Updated May 22,
2019. https://www.aclu.org/cases/sandvig-v-barr-challenge-cfaa
-prohibition-uncovering-racial-discrimination-online.

Shead, Sam. "TikTok Apologizes After Being Accused of Censoring
#BlackLivesMatter Posts." CNBC, June 2, 2020. https://www
.cnbc.com/2020/06/02/tiktok-blacklivesmatter-censorship.html.

Sherwin, Galen, and Esha Bhandari. "Facebook Settles Civil Rights
Cases by Making Sweeping Changes to Its Online Ad Platform."
ACLU, March 19, 2019. https://www.aclu.org/blog/womens
-rights/womens-rights-workplace/facebook-settles-civil-rights
-cases-making-sweeping.

Simonite, Tom. "Congress Is Eyeing Face Recognition, and Companies Want a Say." *Wired,* November 23, 2020. https://www.wired
.com/story/congress-eyeing-face-recognition-companies-want-say/.

Wood, Matt. "Thoughts on Recent Research Paper and Associated
Article on Amazon Rekognition." Amazon Web Services, January
26, 2019. https://aws.amazon.com/blogs/machine-learning
/thoughts-on-recent-research-paper-and-associated-article-on
-amazon-rekognition/.

Yin, Leon, and Aaron Sankin. "Google Blocks Advertisers from
Targeting Black Lives Matter YouTube Videos." Markup, April
9, 2021. https://themarkup.org/google-the-giant/2021/04/09
/google-blocks-advertisers-from-targeting-black-lives-matter
-youtube-videos.

Zhang, Maggie. "Google Photos Tags Two African-Americans as Gorillas Through Facial Recognition Software." *Forbes,* July 1, 2015. https://www.forbes.com/sites/mzhang/2015/07/01/google -photos-tags-two-african-americans-as-gorillas-through-facial -recognition-software/?sh=6ac357c713d8.

ALGORITHMIC ASSAULT

Brandeis Marshall

rtificial intelligence (AI), automated decision-making algorithms, is a new brand of social injustice. AI has infiltrated many sectors and industries as the solution-savant. It's promoted as a way to reduce financial costs by digitizing repeatable mundane tasks and then automating their execution with minimal to no human interaction. But AI bias—created by reflecting and replicating prejudice in public, private, and civic structures into the digital space—squarely puts Black people in danger, danger that scales the breadth and impact of discrimination.

Innocent Black people, such as Nijeer Parks, Robert Julian-Borchak Williams, and countless others whose experiences didn't make the local/national press, are mistreated and then labeled digitally as criminals. Our faces are captured on video surveillance in our local retail store. If a crime is committed at that store, the local police can obtain that video footage and use AI, in the form of facial recognition algorithms, to find likely facial matches. But AI isn't designed to distinguish Black faces like it does white faces, so a facial match of Black people mischaracterizes often. The time lapse to untangle the digital mischaracterization initiated by AI may take hours, days, years, or may never happen. In the face of these dangers, Black people must remain clear and focused on securing our own agency.

One cause for the racism embedded in the technology we use is the lack of conversations between the Black and white technology communities. AI's engineers, architects, and coders are mainly white men who saturate the tech they build with their misconstrued interpretations of Black culture and humanity. The lack of genuine co-creation and collaboration then results in technology applications that are pushed onto the Black community while our explicit needs are overlooked, and then marginalized, to make way for the preferred messaging outlined by the white tech community. What is clear from the current state of messaging surrounding AI is that we can't isolate the AI design, construction, and scaling from the emotional outcomes and social constructs it's invented to reinforce. We also cannot ignore how the lack of Black people involved in conversations with the white tech community runs parallel to the terrorism done digitally to us across different areas of life. Therefore, we need to issue a divorce from the term *AI bias/harms* and, instead, appropriately call what is happening *algorithmic assault.*

The path for algorithmic assault is laid with us being invisible or hypervisible. It's not just death by a thousand paper cuts anymore, it's death by one to a thousand data points as well. We are unaware of assaults that are happening to us online until there's occasion for these algorithmic assaults to impact our physical bodies offline. The truth is, we have misjudged the power, influence, scope, and scale of the algorithmic assault on our lives and in our careers. In the digital space, especially, we follow our oppressor's playbook. We do what we are told: learn how to code, get a tech job, don't leave that tech job, keep the tech job door open for others that look like you, bring in more people that look like you into the tech sphere, become a tech manager, and keep your head low until you are in the power seat or at the power table to "make a difference." Somehow, we've accepted that the Black people's path to digital visibility is through tech careers.

Moving forward, we need to develop digital smarts where we focus on isolating skills and language for understanding and translating how we can navigate our virtual identities just as vehemently as we defend our physical identities. Learning and then adopting digital smarts are a modern necessity for us because we experience algorithmic injustices across industries. We need to build our agency in the historical, political, social, economic, and legal impact of algorithmic thinking, design, implementation, and deployment of digital systems. These digital smarts require us to detail how tech works, particularly in surveillance tech and other automated decision systems, learning project/product management, technical communication, coding, and/or data skills. The path forward right now is that Black people need to dedicate time toward lectures, seminars, workshops, and books that explain the nuances of algorithmic thinking, design, implementation, execution, and impact to non-white communities. It goes to the heart of algorithmic assault and how the most vulnerable communities are affected by technologies.

Furthermore, we need Black people to be educated as digital translators—for those of us who love to code, we do it with a purpose to deeply understand data, algorithms, and technology in digital spaces. By equipping ourselves with these tools, we can then contribute to devising countermeasures to algorithmic assaults. Educational systems must also teach the dehumanizing acrobatics intended to erase Black people's faces, names, lives, and humanity digitally to prepare the next generation for the inevitable future. Finally, we need a sector of Black people to be educated as digital storytellers—for those of us who love to communicate, we do it with an intention to publicly call out and hold societal structures accountable to rectify the social, economic, political, legal, and historical impacts of tech.

Understanding how we are perceived and codified by AI helps us anticipate how algorithms will impact our lives. We can chronicle these algorithmic assaults so that they will not be repeated. Developing ourselves as digital translators and digital storytellers can create a shift in the AI industry. We grow our digital smarts in all places and spaces for racial, gender, and socioeconomic justice, equal pay, health equity, economic security, legal reform, equity in education, business investment, and workplace support. We do this to live in our full dignity openly. We do this to fulfill emancipation's promise of unconditional liberation.

Works Cited

General, John, and Jon Sarlin. "A False Facial Recognition Match Sent This Innocent Black Man to Jail." CNN, April 29, 2021. https://www.cnn.com/2021/04/29/tech/nijeer-parks-facial-recognition-police-arrest/index.html.

Hill, Kashmir. "Wrongfully Accused by an Algorithm." *New York Times,* June 24, 2020. https://www.nytimes.com/2020/06/24/technology/facial-recognition-arrest.html.

Johnson, Khari. "Microsoft Researchers Say NLP Bias Studies Must Consider Role of Social Hierarchies Like Racism." VentureBeat, June 1, 2020. https://venturebeat.com/2020/06/01/microsoft-researchers-say-nlp-bias-studies-must-consider-role-of-social-hierarchies-like-racism/.

Juarez, Jeffrey A., and Kyle D. Brown. "Extracting or Empowering? A Critique of Participatory Methods for Marginalized Populations." *Landscape Journal* 27, no. 2 (2008): 190–204. https://www.jstor.org/stable/43332448?seq=1.

WE'RE TALKING ABOUT AI WRONG

Jordan Harrod

On January 1, 2021, as the AI community went through its nth reckoning on racism, sexism, and algorithmic fairness, I watched researchers, touted as pioneers, disparage the work of others trying to develop equitable systems.

In particular, I listened to the language that opponents to algorithmic fairness research used to distance themselves from any personal responsibility over the algorithms they developed and the power they wield as researchers. Many of them focused on reframing themselves as victims, under attack from "militant liberalism," and framing algorithmic fairness research as factually unfounded political advocacy instead. At the same time, I started to see an increase in reporting on how major AI research companies were advising employees who were filing HR complaints about racial and gender discrimination to receive mental health counseling or take medical leave, without actually addressing the perpetrators of said discrimination. In effect, since entering the field of artificial intelligence, I've watched researchers from marginalized groups be blamed for systemic problems that they did not create and that actively work against them, often as they try to make steps toward improving the system.

Now, this use of language of devaluing algorithmic fairness work is certainly a problem in its own right, but it also highlights a problem with the way algorithms are discussed more broadly. Artificial intelligence models have a well-documented bias problem, and the field as a whole also has a fairly well-documented, but often ignored, language specification problem that detrimentally impacts both the integrity and dialogue surrounding the research and the associated ethical ramifications. This issue is tied to the interdisciplinary nature of artificial intelligence research, which is often derived from fields including computer science, statistics, mathematics, neuroscience, psychology, linguistics, philosophy, economics, and more, where each field has their own terminology set used to describe problems within the scope of the field.

In fact, researchers are increasingly pointing out this issue, often for practical reasons—it is difficult to compare the performance of two systems described using the same language when the underlying definitions are different or not defined at all. Dr. Zachary Lipton, professor of computer science at Carnegie Mellon University, notes this in his coauthored piece "Troubling Trends in Machine Learning Scholarship." Lipton and his coauthors specifically highlight "suggestive definitions, overloaded terminology, and suitcase words" as common examples of language misuse within the field, where *suitcase words* are defined as "words [that] pack together a variety of meanings." For example, the term *bias* can be described as a suitcase word due to its overlapping definitions in legal, statistical, and algorithmic fairness research. Dr. Su Lin Blodgett and her coauthors point out that research on algorithmic bias in the field of natural language processing (NLP), which focuses on developing computer programs to process and analyze human language in a variety of forms, often fails to "engage critically with what constitutes 'bias' in the first place" and that "papers on 'bias' in NLP systems are rife with unstated assumptions about what kinds of system behaviors are harmful, in what ways, to whom, and why." Along this line, Drs. Maximilian Kasy and Rediet Abebe highlight the historical subjectivity behind definitions of fairness in algorithmic research and development in their 2021 paper entitled "Fairness, Equality, and Power in Algorithmic Decision-Making," noting that

> leading notions of fairness take the objective of the algorithm's owner as a normative goal. In the context of hiring, for instance, if productivity is perfectly predictable and an employer's hiring algorithm is profit maximizing without constraints, then their hiring decisions are fair by definition; only deviations from profit maximization are considered discriminatory.

While this issue is tied to the interdisciplinary nature of artificial intelligence research, it is also tied to how algorithmic fairness and bias evaluation is taught in computer science coursework. Inioluwa Deborah Raji, a fellow at the Mozilla Foundation researching algorithmic auditing and evaluation, points out in her coauthored 2021 piece on pedagogy in AI ethics education that research identifying algorithmic fairness and bias concerns in machine learning models is often met with ad hominem attacks claiming that the bias—which has been quantified by said researchers in the same manner as one might characterize any other statistical bias—is in fact a manifestation of laziness fabricated by the researchers themselves, who are often from marginalized groups.

While these discontinuities impact interpretations of research within the field, they also impact public perception of artificial intelligence systems, which, in turn, impacts the progression and deployment of future artificial intelligence research. This is not a particularly new problem—one only has to look at the COVID-19 pandemic to see how the disconnect between scientific and lay interpretations of terms such as *theory* and *hypothesis* impact public opinion on the necessity of public health policies such as stay-at-home orders and social distancing. But even when academically accepted terms are used, definitions may differ between the scientific community and the public. The description of AI systems as "autonomous" and "automated" exemplifies this problem—namely, the term *autonomous* is typically associated by the general public with entities with consciousness and free will, able to make decisions independently based on intrinsic motivations. This contrasts with definitions used by researchers, such as the definition that Drs. Deborah Johnson and Mario Verdicchio propose in their 2017 piece entitled "Reframing AI Discourse":

> Autonomy is a characteristic of artefacts [programs] in which the course of action is established at run time, without human intervention and on the basis of the conditions in the environment in which the artefact [program] operates.

Of course, this issue does not solely stem from within the research community but is also derived from the worlds of consumer marketing and media. Assisted driving systems (Society of Automative Engineers or SAE, Levels 1 and 2) are often branded as "autonomous" in spite of the fact that they do still require human oversight. However, it remains that the public and academic understanding of these terms differ. The fact that the humans behind AI systems—data sources, researchers, developers, and system managers—are typically hidden from the public eye likely adds to this language discrepancy, which then contributes to fears of the technological singularity and loss of control of AI systems.

Addressing the challenge of language underspecification will likely require the development of a set of standards and best practices for artificial intelligence research and communications. This might include leveraging the interdisciplinary nature of artificial intelligence research by reaching out to, collaborating with, and citing researchers in other relevant disciplines (e.g. science and technology studies, history of science, sociology, and epistemology.) with the goal of grounding technical research via existing definitions from other academic disciplines. Additionally, Ms. Raji proposes reforms to educational pedagogy in computer science, including introducing students to related disciplines via assigned reading, inviting speakers from related disciplines, and addressing the implicit positioning of ethics researchers as "lesser" than traditional computer scientists and machine learning researchers.

In addition to these ideas, I believe that explicitly requiring researchers to define terms during the publication process and establishing best practices on public engagement around AI communication will help to address this challenge.

Popular machine learning conferences such as Neural Information Processing Systems (NeurIPS) have recently begun requiring researchers to submit a broader impacts section with their work that addresses the societal impact of the work. The addition of a definitions disclosure for commonly ill-defined terms and clarification of definitions during the peer review process may help reviewers and readers to better understand the framing of the work, improving critiques and allowing the work to reach wider audiences. Looking outside of the academy, and based on past work documenting the effect of public auditing of algorithmic systems on industry norms shifting, researchers might publicly audit the terms used to discuss artificial intelligence to lay audiences and develop best practices toward communicating the impact of these systems in a more effective and accurate manner to lay audiences. This work should be done in partnership and/or under the direction of science communication and science and technology studies researchers, who are trained to perform these types of evaluations within their disciplines already.

Creating such a set of standards will not be easy, and establishing it as a norm for researchers will likely be even harder. The field of artificial intelligence research contains hundreds, if not thousands, of different cultures, each coming with different historical contexts, access to resources, and norms regarding communication. However, it would not be the first time that researchers have had to learn to communicate in new ways, and taking steps toward common definitions will not only support current research progress but will facilitate the exploration of new and diverse ideas that may not have been understood otherwise.

Works Cited

Blodgett, S. L., S. Barocas, H. Daumé III, and H. Wallach. "Language (Technology) Is Power: A Critical Survey of 'Bias' in NLP." *Proceedings of the 58th Annual Meeting of the Association for Computational Linguistics,* 2020: 5454–5476. https://doi.org/10.18653/v1/2020.acl-main.485.

D'Amour, A., K. Heller, D. Moldovan, B. Adlam, B. Alipanahi, A. Beutel, C. Chen, et al. "Underspecification Presents Challenges for Credibility in Modern Machine Learning." 2020. ArXiv:2011.03395 [Cs, Stat]. http://arxiv.org/abs/2011.03395.

Fast, E., and E. Horvitz. "Long-Term Trends in the Public Perception of Artificial Intelligence." 2016. ArXiv:1609.04904 [Cs]. http://arxiv.org/abs/1609.04904.

Garfin, D. R., R. C. Silver, and E. A. Holman. "The Novel Coronavirus (COVID-2019) Outbreak: Amplification of Public Health Consequences by Media Exposure." *Health Psychology* 39, no. 5 (2020): 355–357. https://doi.org/10.1037/hea0000875.

Glaser, A., and C. Adams. "Google Advised Mental Health Care When Workers Complained About Racism and Sexism." NBC News, March 7, 2021. https://www.nbcnews.com/tech/tech-news/google-advised-mental-health-care-when-workers-complained-about-racism-n1259728.

Johnson, D. G., and M. Verdicchio. "Reframing AI Discourse." *Minds and Machines* 27, no. 4 (2017): 575–590. https://doi.org/10.1007/s11023-017-9417-6.

Kasy, M., and R. Abebe. "Fairness, Equality, and Power in Algorithmic Decision-Making." Working paper, October 8, 2020.

Lipton, Z. C., and J. Steinhardt. "Troubling Trends in Machine Learning Scholarship: Some ML Papers Suffer from Flaws That

Could Mislead the Public and Stymie Future Research." *Queue* 17, no. 1 (2019): 45–77. https://doi.org/10.1145/3317287.3328534.

Maurer, M., J. C. Gerdes, B. Lenz, and H. Winner, eds. "Chapter 32: Consumer Perceptions of Automated Driving Technologies: An Examination of Use Cases and Branding Strategies." In *Autonomous Driving.* Berlin: Springer Berlin Heidelberg, 2016. https://doi.org/10.1007/978-3-662-48847-8.

On-Road Automated Driving (ORAD) Committee. "Taxonomy and Definitions for Terms Related to Driving Automation Systems for On-Road Motor Vehicles." SAE International. 2018. https://doi.org/10.4271/J3016_201806.

Raji, Inioluwa Deborah, and Joy Buolamwini. "Actionable Auditing: Investigating the Impact of Publicly Naming Biased Performance Results of Commercial AI Products." *Proceedings of the 2019 AAAI/ACM Conference on AI, Ethics, and Society (AIES '19),* 2019: 429–435. https://doi.org/10.1145/3306618.3314244.

Raji, I. D., M. K. Scheuerman, and R. Amironesei. "You Can't Sit With Us: Exclusionary Pedagogy in AI Ethics Education." *Proceedings of the 2021 ACM Conference on Fairness, Accountability, and Transparency,* 2021: 515–525. https://doi.org/10.1145/3442188.3445914.

Schiffer, Z. "Timnit Gebru Was Fired from Google—Then the Harassers Arrived." Verge, March 5, 2021. https://www.theverge.com/22309962/timnit-gebru-google-harassment-campaign-jeff-dean.

Verma, S., and J. Rubin. "Fairness Definitions Explained." *Proceedings of the International Workshop on Software Fairness,* 2018: 1–7. https://doi.org/10.1145/3194770.3194776.

PART VI

CRIMINAL JUSTICE

Hyper-incarceration is a signature feature of the American criminal justice system. We lock up 1.4 million Americans in state and federal prisons and 738,000 people in local jails, a demographic which is disproportionately Black.

—HEDWIG "HEDY" LEE

Tony McDade. Modesto "Marrero Desto" Reyes. Ruben Smith III. Jarvis Sullivan. Terrell Mitchell. Momodou Lamin Sisay. Derrick Thompson. David McAtee. Tyquarn Graves. Kamal Flowers. Lewis Ruffin Jr. Phillip Jackson. Michael Blu Thomas. Rayshard Brooks. These are just some of the more than two hundred Black people who have been killed at the hands of police since the deaths of George Floyd and Breonna Taylor.

Beyond the historic nationwide protests and seeming solidarity shown by companies and educational institutions alike, the summer of 2020 brought much-needed attention to an endemic problem that has been ongoing for decades. As the essays in this chapter suggest, Black Americans are incarcerated at alarming rates in local, state, and federal prisons as compared to white Americans. The current state of the criminal justice system as a nationwide crisis has already sparked growing movements such as Black Lives Matter and #SayHerName as well as organizations working to understand injustice within the system, including Campaign Zero. It is clear that there is a need for intersectional solutions that address police brutality and mass incarceration's impact on Black families across the country.

There remains a range of opinions about what the next steps will require, as reflected in the Black [CRIMINAL JUSTICE] Agenda, which will cover police abolition, police reform, and mass incarceration's impact on Black women, children, and queer folk:

- Professor **Jamein Cunningham** attempts to dissect the contentious relationship between police and Black Americans by making a case for increasing diversity in police departments as well as making use of technology to limit officer interactions with civilians.

- **Tahir Duckett,** a civil rights attorney, argues that abolition of the carceral system could make room for community engagement efforts that prioritize the well-being of individuals.

- Sociologist **Hedwig Lee** shares the painful realities of Black women who are oftentimes left behind when Black men are disproportionately incarcerated by a broken criminal justice system, and shows how mass incarceration's impact on Black families often goes unseen.

- Organizer and activist **Preston Mitchum** illustrates the relationship between queer Black Americans and the police, drawing on historical turning points with respect to the LBGTQ+ community in the U.S. to argue for abolition as one way to address the reality of the criminal justice system.

NOTHIN' NEW: RACIAL DISPARITIES IN POLICE CONTACT

Jamein Cunningham

The May 2020 killing of George Floyd in Minneapolis sparked the largest civil demonstration against racial injustice and police violence since the 1960s. The national social movement Black Lives Matter (BLM) called for a complete overhaul of the criminal justice apparatus that has destroyed future opportunities for many young Black people. At the forefront of this movement is the contentious relationship between the police and the Black community.

The numbers are alarming. Black men are 2–3 times more likely to be killed by the police compared to white men, and Black women are 1.4 times more likely to be killed by the police relative to white women. Moreover, Black civilians are more likely to have the police draw a gun during an encounter and employ aggressive non–lethal force tactics. Smartphones and social media have captured these aggressive police tactics, broadcasting police misconduct to the masses. And now, racial disparities in police contact and use of force are front and center in national conversation.

Undeniably, racial disparities in police killings of civilians are the direct consequence of racial disparities in police contact and arrests. For example, the New York Police Department is more likely to stop and frisk Black residents and Black people are more likely to be searched and fined by police, arrested—especially for drug offenses—and be involved in traffic stops. Ultimately, these stops do not increase police productivity, as minorities are less likely to be found with contraband and thus equally searching civilians across racial groups would actually result in higher yield.

Given the evidence, it is clear that police protections and the inability to hold police accountable jeopardizes Black lives. Aggressive policing in Black communities and higher rates of lethal force likely stem from protections granted to police officers through the adoption of collective bargaining rights in the 1960s and 1970s. The adoption of bargaining rights and the formation of police unions across U.S. cities occurred during a time of civil unrest in the 1960s. Policing strategies shifted from social control to crime deterrence in Black communities as local governments directed public safety resources toward the influx of Black migrants from the South. Adopting public sector bargaining allowed the police to negotiate provisions that limit disciplinary actions, making it difficult to hold police accountable for illegal activity. Collective bargaining agreements often obtain language that delays investigations of police officers suspected of misconduct or limits the length of investigations. These agreements will regularly prohibit civilian oversight, anonymous civilian complaints, and the participation of nonpolice investigators in misconduct hearings. According to Hickman and Piquero (2009), the percentage of complaints sustained against police officers are lower in police departments where officers can collectively bargain. Rad (2018) finds a strong correlation between police protections in collective bargaining agreements and the number of unarmed civilian deaths by police. That said, the question that we must now answer is how we reform the police to reduce the number of lives lost to police violence.

I propose that police reform should center around increasing diversity within police departments. The Black community has been calling for more representation within police departments since Reconstruction. And the evidence suggests that Black civilians' experiences are different when there is greater diversity within police departments. For instance, Black civilians are arrested less, and minorities are subject to fewer stops when there is more diversity in police departments. Although minority police officers conduct a smaller percentage of vehicle searches, they have greater success rates, suggesting that minority officers are more effective in identifying nonwhite criminals. The police's racial composition and the community they serve have both been shown to influence racial disparities in crime-related outcomes. White officers are more likely to use force and use force more aggressively on minority citizens. More specifically, white officers use force 60 percent more often than Black officers and use gun force twice as often—particularly when dispatched to Black neighborhoods. Both Facchini et al. (2020) and Bulman (2019) find that electing Black sheriffs reduces racial disparities in arrests. The reduction in Black arrests relative to white arrests is driven by how officers handle less serious crimes when police have more discretion in arresting civilians. One example of increasing diversity within police departments resulted in affirmative action plans that increased the share of minority police officers. These police departments not only increased the number of Black police officers but also had lower victimization rates for both Black and white civilians and less police violence directed at minorities.

In addition to increasing diversity, departments should adopt new technology to reduce police contact for actions that typically result in civic infractions or tickets. Too many times, Black lives have been lost due to misunderstandings surrounding traffic violations that escalate to the use of lethal force. President Obama's Task Force on 21st Century Policing also called for the adoption of new technologies such as body cameras to increase transparency and provide context to police-community encounters. In the years following these recommendations, many police departments in urban communities have adopted the use of body cameras. However, the adoption of body cameras has shown to have little influence on police complaints or police use of force. This is in part due to the discretionary decision of individual officers to actually use body cameras. In many instances, police officers fail to turn on their body cameras or begin recording interactions after the initial encounter. However, research has shown that additional training, especially procedural justice training, reduces complaints of aggressive policing. Another solution to consider is the use of automated ticketing systems that can reduce the footprint of the police and reduce officers' discretion when it comes to enforcing traffic laws. Overall, to reduce the unnecessary killings of unarmed civilians, it is fundamental to change the experience that Black people encounter with the police.

Lastly, protections typically associated with police unions have made it exceedingly difficult to hold police accountable for misconduct. Activist organizations, such as Campaign Zero, have long challenged the language and provisions limiting police accountability and have put forth a series of recommendations to improve police-community relations.

Recommendations call for removing waiting periods before interrogations. The waiting periods between incident and interview give officers the time to "huddle" and corroborate stories, obstruct evidence, prepare a statement, and influence public opinion. Recommendations also call for maintaining disciplinary records of police officers, which are often destroyed after a certain length of time. In addition to police union contracts, Law Enforcement Officers' Bill of Rights provide disciplinary protections that supersede union contracts or local provisions related to police employment. These state legislative acts contain language that limits police accountability. Officers' Bill of Rights often contain ambiguous language, limit civilian oversight, and include limitations on retaining disciplinary records of misconduct. Police officers have the right to fair terms of employment. However, their societal standing does not dissolve civilians' rights to protections provided by the Fifth and Fourteenth Amendments. The public's trust in the police is of utmost importance, and police must be held accountable for misconduct. Therefore, reform should involve removing protections that go beyond constitutional rights and limit police accountability.

It is also important to note that many officers, especially in the South, are not protected by collective bargaining agreements or Officers' Bill of Rights but are still shielded through informal channels that limit disciplinary action. This points to a systemic accountability problem. Therefore, police reform should include a new model of policing; a model that does not focus solely on clearance rates and convictions but instead on fairness and justice. Reform should target policing strategies that restore police legitimacy and embrace diversity not only in recruitment but in police tactics and communication.

The racial disparities that exist in the criminal justice system are a by-product of a broader ailment rooted in the historical, political, and economic structures of racial injustice in the United States. Improving police-community relations will not only enhance public safety measures, but also address the long-lasting concerns of the over-incarceration of Black bodies.

Works Cited

Ang, D. "The Effects of Police Violence on Inner-City Students." KS Faculty Research Working Paper Series RWP20–016, June 2020.

Ariel, B., W. A. Farrar, and A. Sutherland. "The Effect of Police Body-Worn Cameras on Use of Force and Citizens' Complaints Against the Police: A Randomized Controlled Trial." *Journal of Quantitative Criminology* 31, no. 3 (2015): 509–535.

Atiba Goff, P., T. Lloyd, A. Geller, S. Raphael, and J. Glaser. *The Science of Justice: Race, Arrests, and Police Use of Force.* Los Angeles: Center for Policing Equity, 2016. https://policingequity.org/images/pdfs-doc/CPE_SoJ_Race-Arrests-UoF_2016–07–08–1130.pdf.

Ba, B., D. Knox, J. Mummolo, and R. Rivera. "Diversity in Policing: The Role of Officer Race and Gender in Police-Civilian Interactions in Chicago." Working paper, 2020.

Buehler, J. W. "Racial/Ethnic Disparities in the Use of Lethal Force by US Police, 2010–2014." *American Journal of Public Health* 107, no. 2 (2017): 295–297.

Bulman, G. "Law Enforcement Leaders and the Racial Composition of Arrests." *Economic Inquiry* 57, no. 4 (2019): 1842–1858.

Cesario, J., D. J. Johnson, and W. Terrill. "Is There Evidence of Racial Disparity in Police Use of Deadly Force? Analyses of Officer-Involved Fatal Shootings in 2015–2016." *Social Psychological and Personality Science* 10, no. 5 (2019): 586–595.

Cheng, C., and W. Long. "The Spillover Effects of Highly Publicized Police-Related Deaths on Policing and Crime: Evidence from Large US Cities." 2018. https://www.lsu.edu/business/economics/files/microecon-conf-tulane-long.pdf.

Close, B. R., and P. L. Mason. "Searching for Efficient Enforcement:

Officer Characteristics and Racially Biased Policing." *Review of Law & Economics* 3, no. 2 (2007): 263–321.

Correll, J., S. M. Hudson, S. Guillermo, and D. S. Ma. "The Police Officer's Dilemma: A Decade of Research on Racial Bias in the Decision to Shoot." *Social and Personality Psychology Compass* 8, no. 5 (2014): 201–213.

Cox, R., and J. Cunningham. "Financing the War on Drugs: The Impact of Law Enforcement Grants on Racial Disparities in Drug Arrests." *Journal of Policy Analysis and Management* 40, no. 1 (2021): 191–224.

Cox, R., J. Cunningham, and A. Ortega. "The Impact of Affirmative Action Litigation on Police Killings of Civilians." Working paper, 2020.

Cunningham, J., D. Feir, and R. Gillezeau. "Collective Bargaining Rights, Policing, and Civilian Deaths." Working paper, 2020.

Cunningham, J. P., and R. Gillezeau. "Don't Shoot! The Impact of Historical African American Protest on Police Killings of Civilians." *Journal of Quantitative Criminology* 37 (2019): 1–34.

Derenoncourt, E. "Can You Move to Opportunity? Evidence from the Great Migration." Working paper, 2019.

Desmond, M., A. V. Papachristos, and D. S. Kirk. "Police Violence and Citizen Crime Reporting in the Black Community." *American Sociological Review* 81, no. 5 (2016): 857–876.

Dharmapala, D., R. H. McAdams, and J. Rappaport. "Collective Bargaining Rights and Police Misconduct: Evidence from Florida." University of Chicago Coase-Sandor Institute for Law & Economics Research Paper, No. 831, 2019.

Donohue, J. J., III, and S. D. Levitt. "The Impact of Race on Policing and Arrests." *Journal of Law and Economics* 44, no. 2 (2001): 367–394.

Edwards, F., M. H. Esposito, and H. Lee. "Risk of Police-Involved

Death by Race/Ethnicity and Place, United States, 2012–2018." *American Journal of Public Health* 108, no. 9 (2018): 1241–1248.

Eriksson, K. "Moving North and into Jail? The Great Migration and Black Incarceration." *Journal of Economic Behavior & Organization* 159 (2019): 526–538.

Facchini, G., B. G. Knight, and C. Testa. "The Franchise, Policing, and Race: Evidence from Arrests Data and the Voting Rights Act." Technical report, National Bureau of Economic Research, 2020.

Feigenberg, B., and C. Miller. "Racial Divisions and Criminal Justice: Evidence from Southern State Courts." Technical report, National Bureau of Economic Research, 2018.

Feigenberg, B., and C. Miller. "Racial Disparities in Motor Vehicle Searches Cannot Be Justified by Efficiency." NBER Working Paper, w27761, 2020.

Friedman, M. L. "Spatial Tests for Racial Bias in the NYPD's Stop, Question & Frisk Program." Working paper, 2017.

Fryer, R. G. "An Empirical Analysis of Racial Differences in Police Use of Force." *Journal of Political Economy* 127, no. 3 (2019): 1210–1261.

Goncalves, F., and S. Mello. "A Few Bad Apples? Racial Bias in Policing." Working paper, 2020.

Harvey, A., and T. Mattia. "Reducing Racial Disparities in Crime Victimization." Working paper, 2019.

Hickman, M. J., and A. R. Piquero. "Organizational, Administrative, and Environmental Correlates of Complaints About Police Use of Force: Does Minority Representation Matter?" *Crime & Delinquency* 55, no. 1 (2009): 3–27.

Hoekstra, M., and C. W. Sloan. "Does Race Matter for Police Use of Force? Evidence from 911 Calls." Working paper, 2020.

Horrace, W. C., and S. M. Rohlin. "How Dark Is Dark? Bright Lights, Big City, Racial Profiling." *Review of Economics and Statistics* 98, no. 2 (2016): 226–232.

Huq, A. Z., and R. H. McAdams. "Litigating the Blue Wall of Silence: How to Challenge the Police Privilege to Delay Investigation." *University of Chicago Legal Forum,* vol. 2016.

Levine, K. "Police Suspects." *Columbia Law Review* 116 (2016): 1197.

MacDonald, J. M., and J. Fagan. "Using Shifts in Deployment and Operations to Test for Racial Bias in Police Stops." *AEA Papers and Proceedings* 109 (2019): 148–151.

Owens, E., D. Weisburd, K. L. Amendola, and G. P. Alpert. "Can You Build a Better Cop? Experimental Evidence on Supervision, Training, and Policing in the Community." *Criminology & Public Policy* 17, no. 1 (2018): 41–87.

Pang, M.-S., and P. A. Pavlou. "Armed with Technology: The Impact on Fatal Shootings by the Police." Fox School of Business Research Paper, 16–020, 2016.

Pierson, E., C. Simoiu, J. Overgoor, S. Corbett-Davies, D. Jenson, A. Shoemaker, V. Ramachandran, P. Barghouty, C. Phillips, R. Shroff, et al. "A Large-Scale Analysis of Racial Disparities in Police Stops Across the United States." *Nature Human Behaviour* 4, no. 7 (2020): 1–10.

Rad, A. N. "Police Institutions and Police Abuse: Evidence from the US." Master's thesis, University of Oxford, Oxford, 2018.

Ross, C. T. "A Multi-Level Bayesian Analysis of Racial Bias in Police Shootings at the County-Level in the United States, 2011–2014." *PLOS ONE* 10, no. 11 (2015): e0141854.

"Stop-and-Frisk Data." 2017. NYCLU. Accessed March 5, 2020.

"Stop-and-Frisk in the De Blasio Era." 2019. NYCLU. Accessed March 5, 2020.

West, J. "Racial Bias in Police Investigations." Working paper, 2018.

Wood, G., T. R. Tyler, and A. V. Papachristos. "Procedural Justice Training Reduces Police Use of Force and Complaints Against Officers." *Proceedings of the National Academy of Sciences* 117, no. 18 (2020): 9815–9821.

Wright, J. E., and A. M. Headley. "Police Use of Force Interactions: Is Race Relevant or Gender Germane?" *American Review of Public Administration* 50, no. 8 (2020): 0275074020919908.

Yokum, D., A. Ravishankar, and A. Coppock. "Evaluating the Effects of Police Body-Worn Cameras." Lab@DC working paper, October 20, 2017.

THE CARCERAL SYSTEM HAS NO FUTURE

Tahir Duckett

I n April 2021, the nation stood on a knife's edge waiting for a verdict in the case of Derek Chauvin, the Minneapolis Police Department officer who killed George Floyd by kneeling on his neck for nine minutes and twenty-nine seconds after Floyd was accused of passing a counterfeit bill at a nearby convenience store. The original police report, signed and affirmed by the other officers on the scene, never mentioned the use of force against Floyd, saying only that he had physically resisted officers and simply "appeared to be suffering medical distress" before he died. But Darnella Frazier, a Black teenager passing by, had filmed the entire encounter, exposing the police report as a lie and leading to the rarest of circumstances: a police officer indicted and tried for murder for killing in the line of duty.

The videotaped murder of Floyd sparked global protests of fifteen to twenty-six million people in the United States alone, the largest movement in the country's history. Millions had seen the video and already rendered their verdict—this killing was unjust. And yet it was far from clear that a jury would convict Chauvin of murder. The truth is that no system with policing and prisons at its heart can regularly deliver justice to Black people, as these institutions are designed to criminalize our existence.

Only 140 police officers were indicted on murder or manslaughter charges between 2005 and 2021, a time period covering over 17,500 police killings. Just 44 of them were convicted of any crime, and only 7 were convicted of murder. The system of laws, investigators, prosecutors, and judges that had failed to punish the killers of Amadou Diallo, Rekia Boyd, Michael Brown, Tamir Rice, and Breonna Taylor now promised us justice. Chauvin's conviction and caging were to be proof that this system could work, that it could be reformed, but it was in truth nothing more than retributive table scraps tossed at our feet to appease our righteous fury. After the verdict was announced, there was no emotional response equal to those weeks of energetic protest. No joy or dancing in the streets. Just a weary sense of relief that this time, just this *once,* an officer would face consequences for murdering one of us.

Efforts to reform the carceral system have generally failed because they rest on an incorrect assumption that it mostly works, that at its root the system is more good than bad, and that if we can get rid of the few bad apple police officers and prison guards, free the few people unjustly imprisoned, or eliminate the cruelest, most torturous, practices in our prisons, the system will serve our needs. This is a critical mistake.

U.S. prisons caged 2.15 million people in 2017. That is more than the entire population of Nebraska and reflects a rate over ten times greater than Denmark or Sweden and nearly nine times greater than Germany. To believe that this system is *almost* just is to believe that the United States is nearly nine times more criminogenic than Germany. Meanwhile, eight hundred thousand people are employed as police officers in the United States, a force that would be the sixth-largest standing army in the world. Police officers kill over one thousand people per year, a per capita rate higher than any other wealthy country in the world. And these deaths are just the tip of the iceberg. Police officers put around eighty thousand people in the hospital every year. Under the ever-present threat of violent enforcement, police officers also harass and interrupt the lives of hundreds of thousands of people every year in myriad other ways: stop-and-frisk, sidewalk interrogations, vehicle searches, search warrants executed on homes, asset forfeiture, and predatory ticketing just to name a few. The countless innocent bystanders caught up in these intrusive tactics have no serious recourse for any damage to their person or property. And this oppressive policing occurs almost exclusively in Black communities that have been segregated from white communities, rendering this violence nearly invisible to the rest of the country.

For all of this, you would hope this nation would have the lowest crime rates in the world. But it does not. Our crime rates are no lower than those in other wealthy countries, and it is no wonder. The carceral system responds to criminal activity, but it does very little to prevent crime. One study estimates that police spend over a third of their time on noncriminal matters, such as helping with keys locked in cars or responding to people who fall ill in public, and only 4 percent of their time on serious violent crime. But the carceral system offers nothing to rectify the social circumstances (e.g., trauma, scarcity, addictions, and other illnesses) that most often lead to criminal behavior in the first place. What's more, evidence continues to accumulate that our approach to policing and incarceration actually can make us *less* safe. High rates of incarceration in neighborhoods break down social and family bonds in communities, making other members of those communities more likely to engage in criminal behavior.

Many believe that the size and nature of the carceral system, while unfortunate, is necessary for either deterrence or retributive punishment, but upon closer look, it is clear that it only responds to a fraction of the most harmful conduct happening in our communities. Of all serious crimes (murder, rape, aggravated assault, burglary, etc.), only about 11 percent result in an arrest, and only about 2 percent end in a conviction. Less than 1 percent of rapes lead to a felony conviction. Only 62 percent of murder cases are ever cleared. Those responsible for devastating losses of wealth in communities across the country during the 2008 financial crisis never faced indictment, let alone prosecution or incarceration. Corporate executives responsible for the pollution and carbon dioxide emissions that are ravaging our planet will never see the inside of a jail cell. Nor will any of the employers responsible for around $15 billion of annual wage theft, which amounts to more stolen property than all the larcenies and burglaries in the United States combined.

This is all by design. The basic ideas and principles undergirding the criminal justice system ensure that it does not and cannot protect Black people. From slave patrols that terrorized enslaved and free Blacks alike to the disproportionate harm inflicted upon Black people by the modern carceral system, there is abundant evidence that the carceral system was specifically designed as a set of tools to control and ultimately destroy Black lives. This same system has incarcerated as many as one in three Black men and one in eighteen Black women. Police occupy and wage war in Black communities in ways unheard of in white communities. Indeed, to imagine policing that does not occupy and terrorize Black neighborhoods or that effectively solves crimes and prevents harms is to imagine a policing that has never existed in this country. Though efforts to reform the carceral system—to make it fairer, more equitable, less violent and cruel—are plentiful, nearly all have come up short. However, where we focus less on reform and more on reducing the size and scope of the system, there is hope.

Across the country, municipalities are beginning to shift certain responsibilities, including mental health crises and traffic enforcement, away from the police toward other responders. Fledgling violence interruption programs have shown great promise in preventing gun violence. Public health researchers have identified consent- and sex-education programs that are highly effective at preventing sexual violence. All these services remain chronically underfunded, attracting only a fraction of the hundreds of billions of dollars spent annually on policing and prisons. Furthermore, strengthening and stabilizing the social safety net can lead to less economic insecurity, another key correlate of criminal activity.

These are the seeds of the future: a world where we invest in efforts to reduce harmful activity, rather than just respond to it. It requires a shift in thinking away from the myth that we can punish our way to a safer society and toward a public safety strategy centered around meeting people's most basic material and physical needs. Instead of spending around $35,000 per year incarcerating someone for theft, we should use that money to make sure they don't need to steal. Instead of criminalizing homelessness by putting people in jail and levying fees for sleeping on park benches or public solicitation, we should leverage the unparalleled wealth and resources of this nation to ensure that people are housed. Increasing access to stable, quality housing can reduce the likelihood of criminal activity and should be seen as a key part of our public safety strategy.

The same is true of increasing access to high-quality mental health resources. We must build a mental health infrastructure that will allow us to begin to take the opportunities to address trauma and neglect before it turns into violence and abuse. The current state of the police system and prisons can't help us get there. We urgently need fewer officers with a narrower scope of work, and we have to start putting non-carceral programs at the center of our strategies for building community safety. We have tried reforming the carceral system, investing in more training and new technology, and asking officers to engage in "community policing." But there's no getting around it—reducing the harm that the carceral system levies upon Black neighborhoods requires reducing the size and scope of that very system. Until we do so, we will never be free.

Works Cited

Asher, Jeff, and Ben Horwitz. "How Do the Police Actually Spend Their Time?" *New York Times,* June 19, 2020. https://www.nytimes.com/2020/06/19/upshot/unrest-police-time-violent-crime.html.

Bandele, Monifa. "Take It from an Activist Who Was There: Stop and Frisk Cost New Yorkers Their Lives." Vox, February 14, 2020. https://www.vox.com/first-person/2020/2/14/21136892/stop-and-frisk-bloomberg-activist.

Baughman, Shima. "Police Solve Just 2% of All Major Crimes." Conversation, August 20, 2020. https://theconversation.com/police-solve-just-2-of-all-major-crimes-143878.

Buchanan, James, et al. "Black Lives Matter May Be the Largest Movement in U.S. History." *New York Times,* July 3, 2020. https://www.nytimes.com/interactive/2020/07/03/us/george-floyd-protests-crowd-size.html.

Burrowes, Kimberly. "Can Housing Interventions Reduce Incarceration and Recidivism?" Housing Matters, February 27, 2019. https://housingmatters.urban.org/articles/can-housing-interventions-reduce-incarceration-and-recidivism.

Cooper, David, and Teresa Kroeger. "Employers Steal Billions from Workers' Paychecks Each Year." Economic Policy Institute, May 10, 2017. https://www.epi.org/publication/employers-steal-billions-from-workers-paychecks-each-year/.

Lopez, German. "The Derek Chauvin Guilty Verdict Is a Huge Outlier." Vox, April 21, 2021. https://www.vox.com/2021/4/21/22395598/derek-chauvin-guilty-verdict-george-floyd-police-shootings.

"Persons Held in Prisons: 2019." United Nations Office on Drugs and Crime. https://dataunodc.un.org/data/prison/persons%20held%20total.

Stemen, Don. "The Prison Paradox: More Incarceration Will Not Make Us Safer." For the Record Evidence Brief Series. 2017.

Weichselbaum, Simone, et al. "Violent Encounters with Police Send Thousands of People to the ER Every Year." Marshall Project, June 23, 2021. https://www.themarshallproject.org/2021/06/23/violent-encounters-with-police-send-thousands-of-people-to-the-er-every-year.

THE INVISIBILITY OF BLACK WOMEN AND THE CONSEQUENCES OF MASS INCARCERATION

Hedwig "Hedy" Lee

While there has been increased bipartisan attention to mass incarceration in the United States and subsequent recent reductions in prison and jail populations, the United States continues to have the highest incarceration rates compared to other high-income countries, and Black, Latinx, and Native American communities continue to be disproportionately impacted. At the current pace of decarceration, it will take twenty-four years for the federal prison population to return to pre–mass incarceration levels, sixty-eight years for state prison populations to return to pre–mass incarceration levels, and nineteen years for the Black incarceration rate to equal the 2019 white incarceration rate.

Poor sanitation, overcrowding, and inadequate access to health care in jails and prisons have amplified the need to reduce jail and prison populations and improve conditions in these institutions. According to data collected by the Marshall Project, at least 1,738 prisoners have died of coronavirus-related causes, and 276,235 people in prison have tested positive for COVID-19, which is about 1 in 5 individuals in prison.

Despite increased attention to mass incarceration and its consequences for racial disparities in health and well-being of men, a crucial piece of the narrative is often missing in our academic and policy conversations: the stories of the wives, mothers, grandmothers, and sisters who take care of and advocate for family members inside and outside prison. Like the many men who are currently incarcerated, these women also face increased health risks that often go undiscussed in policy and public health conversations. A growing body of research links the incarceration of women's family members to their own worsening mental and physical health, often driven by the introduction of numerous chronic social and economic stressors that result when a family member is placed behind bars. These women are often already living in economically disadvantaged communities, frequently the very same communities hit hard by COVID-19. Incarceration of a family member serves to further compound these disadvantages. Despite these realities, the frame we use to understand mass incarceration leaves women out. This is particularly egregious among Black women, over half of whom have at some point had a family member in prison, amounting to almost ten million Black women in total.

When I think about the invisibility of Black women family members in discussions of the collateral consequences of mass incarceration, I often think about a 2015 *Guardian* article that featured an interview with poet Claudia Rankine discussing her fifth book, *Citizen*. In her interview, Rankine noticed the ways in which Black women are erased in the context of police-involved killings of Black civilians:

> I know in the States right now, movements such as Black
> Lives Matter have been grappling with this issue of
> whether those black lives also equal black female lives,

and why the media doesn't focus on the loss of black female lives as much as it focuses on the loss of black men. There are practical reasons," she says. "Race studies professor Kimberlé Crenshaw has talked about how the numbers are just higher for black men. But there is a way in which black women are at the bottom. The invisibility of black women is astounding.

As a Black and Puerto Rican woman professor and someone who studies Black women and their well-being in regard to hyper-incarceration, hyper-policing, and hyper-surveillance, these words are familiar and troubling. I have wondered countless times why Black women are invisible in so many of our academic and political conversations as they relate to mass incarceration. Given the vast number of Black women impacted by the criminal legal system, why do we not recognize them? How can we begin to make Black women visible and center Black women in our social justice frames for policy making and political progress? The answers to these questions are complicated, but not insolvable.

Audre Lorde, in her essay entitled "The Transformation of Silence into Language and Action" in *Sister Outsider,* wrote that "within this country where racial difference creates a constant, if unspoken, distortion of vision, Black women have on one hand always been highly visible, and so, on the other hand, have been rendered invisible through the depersonalization of racism." Melissa Harris-Perry describes this as misrecognition. She sees recognition as integral to citizenship. But Black women who often bear the intersecting burdens of race, gender, and class disparities are often mischaracterized by insidious stereotypes and racial tropes in media and politics, making them both hyper-visible and invisible at the same time. These mischaracterizations disallow for recognition of Black women's humanity and the unique challenges facing Black women.

In regard to the criminal justice system, when Black men are harassed and/or arrested by police, it is Black women who bear the cost of fines, bail, lawyers, and lost wages, as well as experience the psychological toll of constant worry for their well-being. When men are in prison or jail, it is women who organize the visits—sometimes traveling very far away with multiple family members in tow, who put money in commissary accounts, who send food packages, who pay the phone bills, who advocate for family members who get put in solitary or when family members are not getting the medical attention that they require. They are the therapists helping to keep their loved ones behind bars strong and hopeful. They are the social workers keeping families together. They are the nutritionists curating food packages to supplement meager food provided in prison. They do these things because they love fiercely, often at the cost of their own health and well-being. But somehow, we do not see these women nor do we see their love and their labor.

So how can we use this information to center Black women in research practice and policy as it relates to mass incarceration and population health? My interviews with women with incarcerated family members make it clear that the state does not recognize the labor of these women. Prisons and jails would not function without the labor of family members when men are on the inside, keeping them clothed and fed and providing housing and/or other forms of support when they return. We need to tell more stories about women with incarcerated loved ones, like those that Stacey Abrams shared about her younger brother, who cycled in and out of prison due to undiagnosed and untreated mental health issues and drug addiction.

We must believe women. Many of the women I talk to discuss that their stories are ignored or discounted. We must respect that knowledge comes in many forms, and we must use this knowledge for research and to inform policy. Almost any policy impacting those on the inside is felt by those on the outside. We have to understand these policies at the state and federal level and listen to women to understand how these changes will impact them and their families. We can also work together with women as they build political power through advocacy and activism. The Alliance of Families for Justice and the Essie Justice Group are two examples of amazing groups doing this work. Moreover, it is crucial that policies aimed to improve mental and physical health in prisons and jails must also center the women and families connected to those on the inside and those who return home from jails and prisons, especially as more places begin to decarcerate.

If we do not see Black women, we will only serve to multiply the negative impacts of the carceral system on the health and well-being of our population and further amplify the already large racial disparities in health that exist in our country.

Works Cited

Abrams, S. "Justice for Georgia: A Plan for Fairness and Community Safety." Join Stacey Abrams. Retrieved January 6, 2021. https://staceyabrams.com/criminaljusticereform/.

Cocozza, P. "Poet Claudia Rankine: 'The Invisibility of Black Women Is Astounding.'" *Guardian,* June 29, 2015. https://www.theguardian.com/lifeandstyle/2015/jun/29/poet-claudia-rankine-invisibility-black-women-everyday-racism-citizen.

Enns, P. K., Y. Yi, M. Comfort, A. W. Goldman, H. Lee, C. Muller, S. Wakefield, E. A. Wang, and C. Wildeman. "What Percentage of Americans Have Ever Had a Family Member Incarcerated?: Evidence from the Family History of Incarceration Survey (FamHIS)." *Socius* 5 (2019): 2378023119829332. https://doi.org/10.1177/2378023119829332.

Harris-Perry, M. V. *Sister Citizen: Shame, Stereotypes, and Black Women in America.* New Haven, CT: Yale University Press, 2013.

Jones, Alexi. "New BJS Data: Prison Incarceration Rates Inch Down, but Racial Equity and Real Decarceration Still Decades Away." Prison Policy Initiative, October 30, 2020. https://www.prisonpolicy.org/blog/2020/10/30/prisoners_in_2019/.

Lee, H., and C. Wildeman. "Things Fall Apart: Health Consequences of Mass Imprisonment for African American Women." *Review of Black Political Economy* 40, no. 1 (2013): 39–52. https://doi.org/10.1007/s12114-011-9112-4.

Lee, H., C. Wildeman, E. A. Wang, N. Matusko, and J. S. Jackson. "A Heavy Burden: The Cardiovascular Health Consequences of Having a Family Member Incarcerated." *American Journal of Public Health* 104, no. 3 (2014): 421–427. https://doi.org/10.2105/AJPH.2013.301504.

Lorde, A. *Sister Outsider: Essays and Speeches.* New York: Penguin Classics, 1984.

Massoglia, M., and W. A. Pridemore. "Incarceration and Health." *Annual Review of Sociology* 41, no. 1 (2015): 291–310. https://doi.org/10.1146/annurev-soc-073014–112326.

Manson, S., J. Schroeder, D. Van Riper, T. Kugler, and S. Ruggles. *IPUMS National Historical Geographic Information System: Version 15.0.* Minneapolis, MN: IPUMS, 2020. http://doi.org/10.18128/D050.V15.0.

National Academies of Sciences, Engineering, and Medicine. *Decarcerating Correctional Facilities during COVID-19: Advancing Health, Equity, and Safety.* Washington, D.C.: National Academies Press, 2020. https://doi.org/10.17226/25945.

1 in 5 Prisoners in the U.S. Has Had COVID-19, 1,700 Have Died. PBS NewsHour, December 19, 2020. https://www.pbs.org/newshour/health/1-in-5-prisoners-in-the-us-has-had-covid-19–1700-have-died.

"A State-by-State Look at Coronavirus in Prisons." Marshall Project, May 1, 2020. https://www.themarshallproject.org/2020/05/01/a-state-by-state-look-at-coronavirus-in-prisons.

Wildeman, C., J. Schnittker, and K. Turney. "Despair by Association? The Mental Health of Mothers with Children by Recently Incarcerated Fathers." *American Sociological Review* 77, no. 2 (2012): 216–243. https://doi.org/10.1177/0003122411436234.

Williams, J. "Melissa Harris-Perry on Shame-Inducing Stereotypes of Black Women." *Ms.,* September 29, 2011. https://msmagazine.com/2011/09/29/melissa-harris-perry-on-shame-inducing-stereotypes-of-black-women/.

Zeng, Zhen. *Jail Inmates in 2018.* Washington, D.C.: Bureau of Labor Statistics, 2020. https://www.bjs.gov/index.cfm?ty=pbdetail&iid=6826.

QUEER AS IN ABOLISHING THE POLICE: CRIMINAL JUSTICE AND BLACK LGBTQ PEOPLE

Preston Mitchum

LGBTQ people are widely overrepresented in the criminal legal system, starting with youth in the juvenile justice system. Gay, lesbian, and bisexual people are 2.25 times more likely to be arrested than straight people.* Furthermore, a 2019 Prison Policy Initiative (PPI) report highlights the disproportionate harassment and incarceration of LGBTQ people of color. Even during incarceration, LGBTQ people, especially queer women and transgender people, experience inhumane treatment. This is no accident.

Police violence and mistreatment of Black LGBTQ people has catalyzed an ongoing movement for queer and transgender rights in the United States. And as a Black queer man raised in the midwestern region with roots in the South, I know far too well that the police have only continued to hurt bodies like mine throughout history. In my own lived experience and as a policy expert who explores issues of criminalization and over-policing, I've learned that the criminal legal system has a literal and metaphorical chokehold on Black LGBTQ people.

---

* The disparity is heightened when the research is narrowed down to lesbian and bisexual individuals, who are four times as likely to be arrested than straight women.

Research suggests that discrimination and stigma—like family rejection, poverty, unsafe schools, housing insecurity, and employment discrimination—lead to criminalization of queer and transgender people. Black LGBTQ people are impacted by decades-old policies targeting race, gender, class, sexual orientation, and gender identity/expression. This disproportionate treatment became even more pronounced since 2016 under the Trump-Pence administration, where housing discrimination was further enabled, where police violence against journalists was celebrated, and where our military was able to openly discriminate against transgender people who wanted to serve.

Every day, transgender and nonbinary people are mistreated by police. According to the National Center for Transgender Equality's 2015 U.S. Transgender Survey, the last comprehensive survey of such kind, 58 percent of respondents who interacted with police who knew they were transgender experienced mistreatment, including verbal harassment, physical/sexual assault, and being forced to perform sexual acts to avoid arrest. Nearly half of transgender survey respondents said they feel uncomfortable seeking police assistance. Respondents who were held in jail, prison, or juvenile detention in the past year of taking the survey faced high rates of physical and sexual assault by facility staff and other inmates. Nearly one-quarter were physically assaulted by staff or other inmates, and one in five, or 20 percent, were sexually assaulted. Respondents were over five times more likely to be sexually assaulted by facility staff than the U.S. population in jails and prisons, and over nine times more likely to be sexually assaulted by other inmates. This disturbing trend highlights the perpetuation of harm among transgender people by law enforcement. And it doesn't stop there.

Police violence also extends to the bedroom to violate constitutionally protected privacy rights of Black LGBTQ people. Across the United States, many state statutes have punished queer and transgender people for having consensual sex. In *Lawrence v. Texas,* police forcibly entered into the private residence of John Lawrence, a white gay man, one late night and arrested him and Tyron Garner, a Black queer man, for violating a Texas law* forbidding certain intimate sexual conduct among two persons of the same sex. Until 2003, gay sex was unlawful in at least fifteen states, which became the justification for private harassment of queer and transgender people by the police.

Police and prosecutors' offices also double down on stigma by criminalizing Black LGBTQ people living with HIV. According to the Centers for Disease Control and Prevention (CDC), HIV-specific criminalization laws largely refer to the use of criminal laws to penalize perceived or potential HIV exposure; alleged nondisclosure of a person who is knowingly living with HIV prior to sexual contact; or unintentional HIV transmission.

The 2015 case against Michael Johnson, the Black collegiate wrestler also known as "Tiger Mandingo," is an all too perfect example of why HIV criminalization laws are an outdated, racist, and homophobic policing tactic affecting Black LGBTQ

---

* Tex. Penal Code Ann. §21.06(a) (2003). "A person commits an offense if he engages in deviate sexual intercourse with another individual of the same sex." The statute defines "deviate sexual intercourse" as follows: "(A) any contact between any part of the genitals of one person and the mouth or anus of another person; or "(B) the penetration of the genitals or the anus of another person with an object." §21.01(1).

people. Without any questions, the same day Johnson told a former sexual partner he was living with HIV, he was pulled out of his class and led away in handcuffs by the St. Charles Police. He, like others in his situation, was later charged with one count of "recklessly infecting another with HIV" and four counts of "attempting to recklessly infect another with HIV," felonies in Missouri. Johnson was originally sentenced to 30.5 years before a Missouri appeals court overturned the conviction, ruling that the prosecuting attorney failed to disclose evidence in a timely fashion to Johnson's attorney.

HIV criminalization laws have more of an effect on Black queer men and transgender people than anyone else. The CDC notes that a much higher proportion of gay, bisexual, and queer men are living with HIV compared to any other group in the U.S. That means there's also an increased chance of people in these demographics having sexual partners living with HIV and therefore being more impacted by HIV over-policing, from arrest to sentencing. Johnson isn't the first—and won't be the last—LGBTQ person harmed by HIV criminalization laws and incarceration based on medical status and condition.

Make no mistake: law enforcement officers breaking and entering into queer spaces is not only restricted to private residences. For the past six decades, police have also raided LGBTQ bars. Through the late 1960s, police consistently raided gay establishments simply to destroy LGBTQ-friendly spaces. In 1969, hundreds of LGBTQ people of color led the first major action against the NYPD in Greenwich Village at the Stonewall Inn. Stonewall was not the first LGBTQ protest against police raids and law enforcement brutality. In 1959, the Cooper Donuts Riot was a small uprising in Los Angeles in response to police harassment. In 1966, at Compton's Cafeteria, LGBTQ people, and transgender individuals in particular, fought back against police violence after vehement anti-trans harassment. And in 1967, after undercover LAPD police officers entered the Black Cat Tavern and started beating LGBTQ patrons, there was a civil demonstration of two hundred attendees.

And these targeted LGBTQ raids are not simply a thing of the past. In 2020, Bryan Smith, co-owner of the Blazing Saddle, Des Moines's long-standing LGBTQ bar, said police raided his business during racial justice uprisings. Though police now walk with queer people at Pride, many LGBTQ organizers actively resist their presence at LGBTQ events. And from 2021 to 2025, New York City law enforcement officers will not march in the parade for the first time since about 1981, and there will be a reduced police presence at events.

LGBTQ people need safer spaces in private and public. One way to make that happen is with fewer police interactions. But the lack of safe, free housing prevents that, and it often leaves young Black and Brown LGBTQ people on the street, leading to more interactions with police. In *Voices from the Street: Survey of Youth Homelessness by Their Peers,* 75 percent of youth experiencing homelessness report regular or negative interactions with police. Of that, an estimated 20 percent reported negative interactions once or twice per month. The causes of homelessness vary, but experts agree that some of the same factors that characterize homelessness are then criminalized by the laws police enforce.

At the same time we're witnessing a resurgence of the fight for Black lives, we have also recognized the intersection of police violence and Black LGBTQ people. And in the wake of the death of George Floyd in Minneapolis, a movement to defund the police captured international attention. It's a clear demand to cut funding and resources from police departments and other law enforcement (even down to zero dollars) and instead invest in programs, services, and interventions that actually make our communities safer. In what ways, we must ask, can we invest in communities and provide resources so crime, however defined, wouldn't occur in the first place? Ending criminalization of Black LGBTQ people will require on-the-ground activism coupled with broad social and policy changes, including but not limited to:

- Investment in Black-led research, advocacy, and grassroots organizations doing work on HIV prevention, treatment, and care.
- State, local, and federal governments grant dollars allowing Black LGBTQ people to open, own, and operate bars and restaurants and create safe and affirming spaces.
- Incentivizing businesses that are also invested in training management and staff on issues impacting our community, like state and interpersonal/patriarchal violence that often happens in bars and restaurants.
- Increasing social support programs and mental health resources for LGBTQ youth within families, schools, communities, and other institutions.
- Investing local, state, and federal dollars in unarmed mediation and intervention teams, the decriminalization of crimes of poverty and survival, transformative justice, community accountability, and real mental health care services.

Abolition of law enforcement is the ultimate goal to protect the lives of Black LGBTQ people. Defunding will free the necessary funds to invest in many vital things that will curb state and interpersonal violence before it occurs. We must start by understanding we don't need cops in the first place, but rather a community that will invest in Black LGBTQ people every day.

Works Cited

Alfonseca, Kiara. "Why the LGBTQ Community Sidelines Police for Pride." ABC News, May 29, 2021. https://abcnews.go.com/US/lgbtq-community-sidelined-police-pride/story?id=77880436.

Bailey, Peggy, and Anna Bailey. "Trump Administration's Proposed Rule Would Perpetuate Racist and Discriminatory Housing Practices." Center on Budget and Policy Priorities, October 18, 2019. https://www.cbpp.org/research/housing/trump-administrations-proposed-rule-would-perpetuate-racist-and-discriminatory.

Berstein, Nell, and Lisa K. Foster. *Voices from the Street: A Survey of Homeless Youth by Their Peers.* Sacramento: California Research Bureau, 2008. https://www.issuelab.org/resources/11579/11579.pdf.

Duran, Leo. "Stonewall Riots Grab the Spotlight from Black Cat Protests." NPR, February 13, 2017. https://www.npr.org/2017/02/13/514935126/stonewall-riots-grab-the-spotlight-from-black-cat-protests.

Abolitionist Policy Changes to Demand from Your City Officials. #8toAbolition. https://www.8toabolition.com/.

Gomez, Amanda Michelle, and Laura Hayes. "Nellie's Sports Bar Security Dragged a Black Woman Down the Stairs. Her Family Is Now Pursuing a Civil Claim." *Washington City Paper,* June 14, 2021. https://washingtoncitypaper.com/article/519364/nellies-sport-bar-security-dragged-a-black-woman-down-the-stairs-her-family-is-now-pursuing-a-civil-claim/.

"HIV and STI Criminalization Laws." Centers for Disease Control and Prevention, December 21, 2020. https://www.cdc.gov/hiv/policies/law/states/exposure.html.

"HIV Surveillance Report: Diagnoses of HIV Infection in the United States and Dependent Areas, 2018." Centers for Disease Control and Prevention, May 2020. https://www.cdc.gov/hiv /library/reports/hiv-surveillance/vol-31/index.html.

Jackson, Hallie, and Courtney Kube. "Trump's Controversial Transgender Military Policy Goes into Effect." NBC News, April 12, 2019. https://www.nbcnews.com/feature/nbc-out /trump-s-controversial-transgender-military-policy-goes-effect -n993826.

James, S. E., J. L. Herman, S. Rankin, M. Keisling, L. Mottet, and M. Anafi. *Executive Summary of the Report of the 2015 U.S. Transgender Survey.* Washington, DC: National Center for Trans-gender Equality, 2016. https://transequality.org/sites/default/files /docs/usts/USTS-Executive-Summary-Dec17.pdf.

Johnson, George M. "Pride Is and Always Was About Rebellion, This Year More Than Ever." Them, June 1, 2020. https://www .them.us/story/this-year-pride-is-about-rebellion.

Jones, Alexi. "Visualizing the Unequal Treatment of LGBTQ People in the Criminal Justice System." Prison Policy Initiative, March 2, 2021.https://www.prisonpolicy.org/blog/2021/03/02/lgbtq/.

Lawrence v. Texas, 539 U.S. 558 (2003).

Movement Advancement Project and Center for American Progress. *Unjust: How the Criminal Justice System Fails LGBT People.* Boulder, CO: Movement Advancement Project, 2016. https://www .lgbtmap.org/file/lgbt-criminal-justice.pdf.

"Police Raid LGBTQ Bar During Des Moines Protests." KCRG, June 8, 2020. https://www.kcrg.com/2020/06/08/police-raid -lgbtq-bar-during-des-moines-protests/.

Solender, Andrew. "Trump Says Police Violence Against Journalists Is 'Actually a Beautiful Sight.'" *Forbes,* September 22, 2020. https://www.forbes.com/sites/andrewsolender/2020/09/22

/trump-says-police-violence-against-journalists-is-actually-a
-beautiful-sight/?sh=2190e44557d6.

Thrasher, Steven. "HIV Conviction of 'Tiger Mandingo' Has Been
Thrown Out." BuzzFeed, December 20, 2016. https://www
.buzzfeednews.com/article/steventhrasher/tiger-mandingos-hiv
-conviction-has-been-thrown-out#.eoLEyQ0P.

Thrasher, Steven. "How College Wrestling Star 'Tiger Mandingo'
Became an HIV Scapegoat." BuzzFeed, July 7, 2014. https://
www.buzzfeed.com/steventhrasher/how-college-wrestling-star
-tiger-mandingo-became-an-hiv-scap.

Villarreal, Daniel. "Before Stonewall, There Was the Cooper's Donuts and Compton's Cafeteria Riots." Queerty, October 7, 2011.
https://www.queerty.com/before-stonewall-there-was-the-coopers
-donuts-and-comptons-cafeteria-riots-20111007/2.

PART VII

ECONOMY

*We need new economic principles, ones that offer some-
thing better than the false scarcity narratives that have
made all of us sicker and poorer while enriching the
wealthy, white few—who have been able to use their
positions of power to make the deliberate policy choices
that brought us to where we are.*

—KYLE K. MOORE

In recent U.S. history, the economic reality of Black and Brown
communities has been dire, to say the least. In 2020, with
most of the world on lockdown, booming businesses came to a
halt, with Black businesses being hit disproportionately. After
the November 2020 elections, economic recovery efforts at
the intersection of racial justice in response to the pandemic
became a top priority, with Biden appointing multiple Black
leaders into key economic positions. For economists, the
schism created by the pandemic offered an opportunity to put
forth bold economic policies that aim to center the experiences
of Black workers across the country. In the Black [ECONOMIC]
Agenda, readers will learn from:

- Macroeconomics professor **Karl Boulware,** who provides
  recommendations to the Federal Reserve about how its
  monetary policy and framework must center Black workers
  to ensure lasting economic recovery.

- Economist **Kyle Moore,** who makes the case for
  stratification economics, a non-neoclassical field of

economics, which houses the economic journey of Black Americans while drawing on history, sociology, and progressive thought. He argues that using an economic framework like stratification gives us full context surrounding the economic reality of Black Americans.

- U.S. Department of Labor chief economist and chief legal counsel **Janelle Jones** and **Angela Hanks,** respectively, who illustrate and propose a bold framework that pushes for refocusing economic recovery efforts on uplifting Black women, appropriately named Black Women Best. Jones recently made history as the first Black woman to hold the post at the Department of Labor.

HOW THE FEDERAL RESERVE
CAN HELP BLACK WORKERS

Karl David Boulware

For U.S. monetary policy, better understanding of the relationship between workplace discrimination and economic growth has led to a much-needed revision of the Federal Open Market Committee's (FOMC)* *Statement on Longer-Run Goals and Monetary Policy Strategy.*** The change to the existing framework, which was made effective in 2020, states that the Federal Reserve is now committed to reducing disparities in the labor market. And with that in mind, the FOMC aims for an economic recovery that is as broad-based and inclusive as possible. Ultimately, what the FOMC's new revision suggests is that the next economic recovery not only has the potential to bring more and better job opportunities in the short run but also ensure long-term employment.

That said, the lack of equitable economic opportunities in the labor market, currently, constrains people from investing in future economic opportunities like starting a business, paying for school, or buying stock. If these inequalities are systemic,

---

* The FOMC is a committee within the Federal Reserve System in charge of U.S. monetary policy.

** *The Statement on Longer-Run Goals and Monetary Policy Strategy* summarizes the framework currently in use by the FOMC to achieve its long-run goals of maximum employment and price stability.

then the national economy will grow less than it should, over time, resulting in a lower future standard of living for all citizens. Macroeconomic policies that promote equal economic opportunity in the short term are also likely to enhance the economy's long-term growth.

What underlies the COVID-19 recession is a major public health crisis. What we've learned is that no amount of monetary stimulus is going to convince consumers to spend money on restaurants and destination vacations if they feel unsafe. So, while monetary policy may help generate better macroeconomic outcomes for Black Americans once the economic recovery is well underway post–health crisis, it can only go so far. A full recovery will depend on vaccinating the population, followed by the FOMC continuing to support the economy to ensure that all workers continue to have equality of opportunity even after the recession is over.

In the labor market, one explanation of well-documented observed economic disparities is race-based employment discrimination. Economically, companies will not be able to afford to discriminate if they have to compete for workers as they would when jobs are plentiful. Therefore, other things being equal, they will be less likely to discriminate against an individual in an economic expansion—when the cost of searching for a qualified replacement is too high.

Accordingly, claims of race-based discrimination will vary over time as a function of the unemployment rate. When a recession hits, the unemployment rate for Black Americans rises more, and at a faster rate, than for white Americans. In a subsequent economic recovery, Black workers find fewer job opportunities than white workers, leading to a smaller and slower decline in unemployment rates. Recent findings also support the idea that employers who engage in racial discrimination in the workplace choose to do so systematically during economic recessions and expansions.

As a result, under the old policy framework, the FOMC would look to slow the economy down well before marginalized workers could experience the full benefit of an economic expansion. Because the old framework doesn't account in any way for the economic consequences of racial discrimination, it also doesn't account for any interaction between monetary policy and racial discrimination in the labor market. Accordingly, the old framework can be viewed as a contributing factor to the slow growth in the number of jobs and ongoing inequalities for Black Americans in the labor market.

The new framework defines *maximum employment* as the highest level of employment that does not cause the prices of basic goods to rise uncontrollably. By defining maximum employment in this way, the FOMC's new framework is enhancing equal opportunity by including broader labor market indicators, especially those measuring labor market disparities.

The motivation for the framework review came from the FOMC's experience presiding over the longest recorded period of economic growth in U.S. history (June 2009–February 2020). One important lesson from this expansion is that when the U.S. economy is growing slowly, monetary policy is ineffective. Therefore, the FOMC can allow the economy to grow for much longer than they could under the old framework.

The FOMC's new framework is also an attempt to replicate the increasing gains in employment experienced by Black Americans and other underrepresented groups during the most recent, record-setting expansion. By incorporating broad labor market indicators in the implementation of monetary policy, the Federal Reserve is supporting a labor market that is less impacted by the structural barriers facing Black workers, while at the same time raising the long-run welfare of all U.S. citizens.

When the COVID-19 recession began, its initial impact between February and April was concentrated in spending on services, a sector where Black businesses are overrepresented. As one would expect, Black business owners saw a decline of 19 percent more than the overall decline in small business owners. Almost twelve months later, the recovery continues to be uneven. In the labor market, employment fell more sharply for Black workers than aggregate employment. These job losses can be explained in part by the saturation of Black Americans working in jobs that have high levels of interpersonal contact and/or a workplace environment that poses greater risk of infection than other jobs.

Because the FOMC has been following the new framework since the beginning of the COVID recession, all the policy tools at the FOMC's disposal are being employed to combat the ongoing economic damage. The FOMC's new framework can support the recovery, but alone, it cannot ensure recovery can continue.

While the Federal Reserve's new framework has the potential to create, indirectly, a more equitable workplace experience for Black American workers, the FOMC's expectation of a more inclusive and broad-based recovery may be unrealistic unless a majority of Americans are vaccinated and the policy of maximum employment continues well after the COVID recession ends. The longer this takes, the less likely this generation of Black workers and business owners will be able to take full advantage of the potential long-run economic outcomes that the new framework can generate.

Works Cited

Boulware, Karl David, and Kenneth N. Kuttner. "Labor Market Conditions and Charges of Discrimination: Is There a Link?" *AEA Papers and Proceedings* 109 (2018): 166–170. doi: 10.1257/pandp.20191086.

Brainard, Lael. "Achieving a Broad Based and Inclusive Recovery." Federal Reserve, October 21, 2020. https://www.federalreserve.gov/newsevents/speech/brainard20201021a.htm.

Brainard, Lael. "Full Employment in the New Monetary Policy Framework." Federal Reserve, January 13, 2021. https://www.federalreserve.gov/newsevents/speech/brainard20210113a.htm.

Clarida, Richard H. "The Federal Reserve's New Framework: Context and Consequences." Federal Reserve, January 13, 2021. https://www.federalreserve.gov/newsevents/speech/clarida20210113a.htm.

Cortex, Guido Matias, and Eliza C. Forsythe. "Heterogeneous Labor Market Impacts of the Covid-19 Pandemic." Upjohn Institute Working Paper 20–327, Kalamazoo, MI, 2020. doi: 10.17848/wp20–327.

Fairlie, Robert W. "The Impact of COVID-19 on Small Business Owners: Evidence of Early Stage Losses from the April 2020 Current Population Survey." National Bureau of Economic Research Working Paper Series, No. 27309, 2020. doi: 10.3386/w27309.

FOMC Statement on Longer-Run Goals. Washington, D.C.: Federal Open Market Committee, January 13, 2021. https://www.federalreserve.gov/monetarypolicy/files/FOMC_LongerRunGoals.pdf.

Rodgers, William M., III. "Race in the Labor Market: The Role of Equal Employment Opportunity and Other Policies." *RSF: The Russell Sage Foundation Journal of the Social Sciences* 5, no. 5 (2019): 198–220. https://doi.org/10.7758/RSF.2019.5.5.10.

THE CASE FOR STRATIFICATION ECONOMICS

Kyle K. Moore

Wealth represents perhaps the greatest axis of economic inequality between Black and white American families, with Black families owning just thirteen cents of wealth for every dollar white families own. The Black unemployment rate has been almost consistently double the white rate over the past fifty years, mostly breaking trends in the face of sharp economic downturns, but always returning to its historical norm. In this most recent pandemic recession beginning in March 2020, for example, the Black-white unemployment ratio fell to just 1.2; however, that ratio climbed in the following months and sits at 1.83 as of April 2021. Black families are almost always more than twice as likely to live below the poverty line as white families, and Black children are three times as likely as white children to live in poverty across the board.

Providing an explanation for these stark and persistent disparities has been a project of social scientists for generations. Stratification economics offers a new approach to understanding these disparities and how to solve them. It stands apart from more mainstream explanations of racial inequality in that it does not treat racial inequality as arising from individual or cultural failures on the part of Black people. Instead, stratification economics points toward the structural features of the U.S. economy, our economic history, and the dynamics of group-based rationality that maintain disparities between privileged and disadvantaged groups. Because of this broader framework, the solutions to racial inequality that stratification economists provide can focus on fixing the systems that generate inequality, rather than fixing Black people. In what follows, I make the case that stratification economics is a superior method of understanding the persistence of racial economic disparities as compared to neoclassical economics and improves on the historical lens brought to those disparities by Marxian political economy.

In neoclassical economic theory, the tradition most economists were trained in throughout the twentieth century, racial differences in incomes were understood as largely determined by differences in the skill levels (human capital) that different racial groups bring to market. Wage differences between similarly skilled workers can be explained in one of two ways: either the employer or other employees at the firm have an irrational distaste for working with members of the group being discriminated against and demand more compensation to put up with doing so (taste-based discrimination); or because the employer lacks enough information to determine how productive a person will be when they hire them, they decide to pay new employees based on a statistical judgment of the person's group's productivity (statistical discrimination).

For neoclassical economists, the market is enough to get rid of any *undeserved* racial inequality. If wage disparities between groups persist over long periods of time, those differences reflect real differences in productivity between those groups.

Racial inequality has indeed been persistent across the history of the United States economy; therefore, following the logic of the neoclassical framework, much of the inequality we observe between Black and white workers supposedly results from skill deficiencies on the part of Black workers.

Neoclassical explanations for *why* the supposed differences in skills and productivity exist differ, but most point toward the educational achievement gap between Black and white Americans as a root cause. The gap in educational attainment is often attributed to a lack of cultural importance placed on education within the Black community, with explanations ranging from the idea that academic achievement is associated with whiteness (the "acting white" hypothesis), to a learned set of low expectations for the future that undervalues investments that may pay off later on (the "culture of poverty" hypothesis).

When observing Black Americans in "poor" economic and social circumstances relative to their white peers, the policy solution from the neoclassical economist is to adjust Black individuals' behaviors and preferences, or Black culture writ large, such that Black people make better choices. For those unfamiliar with the common assumptions made within the neoclassical framework, the conclusions derived from the neoclassical economics of race may seem surprising. Scholars from other disciplines often recoil when persistent racial disparities are characterized as the result of Black cultural and human capital deficits. These ideas find an audience among neoclassical economists because, at its core, neoclassical economics focuses on the individual decision-maker.

Two responses to the neoclassical economics of race exist within the discipline of economics, one older and one relatively new: these are Marxian political economy and stratification economics. In many ways, the two approaches are connected and complementary in providing an alternative way to understand persistent racial disparities. Both approaches take issue with the individualistic focus of the neoclassical approach, contending instead that *social relationships* provide the foundation for economic activity within capitalist economies. Both also exhibit a respect for the role of *history* in shaping race relations and racial socioeconomic disparities. Where stratification economics improves upon the Marxian approach is in its understanding of how and why racial disparities are maintained, and what can be done to disrupt those self-reinforcing processes.

Marxian political economists understand persistent racial inequality to be a by-product of capitalism given the racist history of the United States. America was founded as an economy dependent on the violent theft of Native American land and African labor. Even after slavery was abolished, existing tensions between Black and white workers could be exploited by a mostly white class of employers to keep workers separated and bargaining power low. Within Marxian political economy, racial inequality is just one axis among many that employers exploit to reduce the power of labor.

Scholars in the Marxian tradition are wary of race-specific approaches to solving racial disparities and even of focusing on closing racial gaps as a long-term goal in and of itself. In a worst-case scenario, an exclusive focus on racial disparities could result in a simple reproduction of the existing class structure, though with proportional representation of Black capitalists also exploiting workers.

Both the neoclassical economics of race and Marxian political economy struggle to explain the importance that many white Americans place on their position of *relative advantage* with respect to non-white (and particularly Black) Americans. Both view identity-related concerns as irrational, either from the perspective of individual gain (neoclassical) or broader class solidarity (political economy). But an examination of the history of the United States shows that even long after slavery ended, there have been social and material benefits that redound to membership in one of the dominant identity groups—whether that be whiteness, maleness, protestant Christianity, or others.

Stratification economics was developed as a direct response to the failures of the neoclassical economics of race to account for the persistence of racial inequality. It also goes beyond the analysis of Marxian political economy in understanding the importance of group identity to one's economic and social position. Stratification economics accounts for the importance of maintaining and promoting relative position for members of advantaged groups, and analyzes the effects of that process on the persistence of inequality between groups. While the seeds of the stratification approach can be traced back to sociologist Herbert Blumer and development economist Arthur Lewis (the first and only Black economist so far to win the Nobel in economics), the field came into fruition as a subdiscipline within economics through the work of William "Sandy" Darity, Darrick Hamilton, Rhonda Williams, Patrick Mason, James Stewart, and others over the past two decades.

There are two ideas at the core of stratification economics: that persistent group-based disparities are rational from the perspective of dominant groups and that those disparities provide dominant group members with a slew of social and material benefits—even across class. From this perspective, the answer to the question of how and whether class solidarity among Black and white workers will actually benefit white workers is ambiguous; while an increase in bargaining power could potentially result in absolute benefits in terms of wages and working conditions, the flattening of occupational and relational differences across race would make the loss of relative position a certainty. Racism is not a simple expression of distaste between groups but an expression of the desire to maintain superior group position. It is a tool accessible not only by capitalists seeking to keep the working class at bay but by all those seeking the benefits of whiteness in the United States, whether through full participation in it or adjacency to it.

Stratification economics challenges the framing of Black poverty as the natural result of Black cultural preference for leisure or undervaluation of education. Stratification economics pushes against the attempt to absolve policy makers from the responsibility of rectifying past injustices through policy.

To describe Black poverty as merely a consequence of a racist past and lack of class solidarity without acknowledging what social and material benefits redound to whiteness *today* is to misunderstand the political economic motivations of American conservatism and how that racist history came about in the first place and how it continues today. To understand Black poverty, truly, is to understand what it means to be white in this country and what rights and privileges come with that identity. Ultimately, narratives that shift the responsibility of addressing racial disparities onto the Black community itself, rather than discriminating employers, racist citizens, or an at best indifferent set of institutions, work to reinforce the political economic value of white American identity and adjacency to it relative to Blackness.

The value of stratification economics, particularly for understanding racial disparities in the twenty-first-century United States, is that it can accurately diagnose the source of those disparities and what causes them to persist and point us toward how we must change our narratives and institutions to move beyond them.

AMERICA'S BEST DEPENDS ON BLACK WOMEN BEST

Angela Hanks and Janelle Jones

The COVID-19 pandemic and subsequent recession have inflicted deep wounds, which, left untreated, may never fully heal. The mass illness and death, along with an economy that struggled to provide for millions of families in a crucial time, suggest we will bear the scars of this crisis for years to come. Furthermore, this crisis is magnified for Black women who must face the dual discrimination of sexism and racism, which is often larger than the sum of their parts. We can build a stabler and more resilient economy—one that is equitable and just—by centering Black women in our policy making.

Decades of disinvestment, allegiance to markets (when convenient), and rampant inequality made the COVID recession nearly inevitable—and made it so much worse when it came. Yet while the source of the subsequent widespread economic insecurity was new, the pain is all too familiar to marginalized people in this country, particularly Black women.

The pandemic further exposed and entrenched deep structural flaws in our economy and inequities across race, gender, and class. Women have disproportionately suffered pandemic-related job losses since the start of the crisis. Black women's strong attachment to the labor force has left them especially vulnerable to this economic downturn. Prior to the crisis,

Black women already faced higher unemployment rates than their white counterparts, as well as lower wages, less wealth, and numerous disparities in health care access and treatment. Black women's work is widely devalued in the labor market as they face lower wages and occupational segregation that pushes them into jobs that historically pay less. Black women are disproportionately employed in low-wage jobs with no benefits.

The economic harm inflicted on Black women during this crisis is in many ways a microcosm of the economic harm inflicted on Black women even under the best economic conditions. Black women have long been both the subjects of deprivation in this country and used as a tool by which to justify mass deprivation of others—whether as domestic workers denied basic protections on the job or mothers whose mere existence was used to justify massive cuts in public investment since the 1970s.

Both this moment and the perpetual crisis Black women in this country face are the direct result of intentional policy choices, more often than not made by people who are wealthier, whiter, and more powerful, who seek to concentrate that power in the hands of a few at the expense of all of us. Anti-Black narratives have shaped much of the policy choices that made this economic crisis so acute and so painful for many. Policy failures like mass unemployment stemming from a lack of worker power, and the lack of continued relief to support struggling families, are fueled by a familiar scarcity narrative—that there isn't enough to go around, therefore only a deserving few are entitled to scarce resources.

The crisis has made it painfully clear that getting back to "normal" is not good enough. The legacy of economic exclusion of Black women is woefully long and staggeringly expensive. Economist Michelle Holder estimates that the interaction of gender and racial wage gaps cost Black women $50 billion in 2017 alone. We need a new economic principle, one that centers the most marginalized groups and structures policy decisions in a way that seeks to close, not maintain or deepen, structural inequities. Therefore, we propose using the economic fortunes of Black women as the metric for whether the economy is performing.

Black Women Best posits that if Black women can one day thrive in the economy, then it must finally be working for everyone. If policy makers can reorient their thinking to put Black women first and promote policies that focus on pulling Black women out of the recession and into prosperity, everyone will be lifted up in the process. A "Black Women Best" ideology would lead to enacting deliberate strategies of inclusion to create a stronger economy so that our most marginalized can thrive. In practice, that means taking two crucial steps: first, examining the specific barriers to economic thriving that Black women face, and second, developing policies that are explicitly designed to remove those obstacles.

Applying a Black Women Best framework, policy makers seeking to improve the quality of the labor market overall should, for example, examine why Black women are paid so much less for their labor and address those specific barriers. If employment discrimination is a culprit, policy makers should seek to strengthen worker protections and increase enforcement when employers violate workers' rights. If a lack of bargaining power is partially to blame, policy makers should make it easier for workers to unionize, especially workers in fields where Black women dominate, like care work. If wages are still too low in industries where Black women are overrepresented—again, care work provides a useful example—then policy makers should design care policies that are both intended to increase the availability of care and the wages of those doing the work. Ultimately, all workers benefit from higher wage floors, a more equitable power balance on the job, and robust labor law enforcement. The same principle can be applied across a whole host of policy areas, from housing, to health care, and education.

Policy makers are often all too eager to end emergency programs and declare "mission accomplished" before crises are over, which always leaves Black workers and families behind and in turn weakens the economy overall. But by targeting those who historically have been left behind, we can ensure that everyone gets lifted up. As policy makers work to pull our economy back from the brink, they should make sure they are facilitating a race-inclusive recovery—and not leaving Black workers and families even further behind.

Policy makers cannot—as they did during the last recession—allow relief efforts to subside as the top-line economic indicators improve while ignoring how Black women specifically are faring in the economy. We have tried that too many times to the same result: Black women get left behind, and the economy does not get the sustained relief it needs. Policy makers should instead tie ongoing relief to the economic outcomes of Black workers.

For example, increasing worker power, in the form of sectoral bargaining and labor law reform, will have a disproportionate impact on Black women. Sectoral bargaining provides wage floors and contract coverage across an industry. It is particularly useful for fissured workplaces, misclassified workers, and disaggregated industries like domestic work, in which Black women and other workers of color are disproportionately represented. Long-standing labor laws, including the National Labor Relations Act (NLRA) and the Fair Labor Standards Act (FLSA), created protections for employees and collective bargaining and a floor for wages and benefits. They also intentionally excluded the predominantly Black occupations of domestic workers and agricultural workers, who today are still left out of some federal protections.

The American economy was built on a racist foundation, one that relied on the exploitation of Black women, who even today face steep barriers to economic thriving. While the impact racist policies have had on Black women alone is reason enough to take swift action to address the harm, we also know that it is not only Black women who are impacted by policies of exclusion and extraction. The COVID-19 pandemic has exposed the extent to which an economy that is built on such policies is one that is designed to fail. As policy makers seek to address this crisis, they must examine how we got here. Black Women Best provides perhaps the clearest path to widespread economic well-being and racial justice, finally.

Works Cited

Holder, Michelle. "The 'Double Gap' and the Bottom Line: African American Women's Wage Gap and Corporate Profits." Roosevelt Institute, March 31, 2020. https://rooseveltinstitute .org/publications/the-double-gap-and-the-bottom-line-african -american-womens-wage-gap-and-corporate-profits/.

Insight Center for Community Economic Development. "Centering Blackness: The Path to Economic Liberation for All." Medium, June 18, 2020. https://medium.com/economicsecproj /centering-blackness-the-path-to-economic-liberation-for-all -f6c2c7398281.

PART VIII

PUBLIC POLICY

While all Americans are bearing the harsh brunt of the pandemic, evidence of aggravated racial and ethnic inequalities make even more transparent the necessity of a bold and transformative policy agenda in America.

—WILLIAM "SANDY" DARITY JR.

In a way, *The Black Agenda* is one big policy proposal inclusive of bold ideas as told through the lens of Black experts, communicators, activists, and organizers. What 2020 made clear, especially in light of President Biden's presidential win, is that Black Americans should be at the forefront of policies that ensure the nation's future. Even more importantly, policies made in D.C. and beyond should prioritize and recognize the role systemic racism has had and continues to have in the lives of Black people.

What the Black [POLICY] Agenda will require is a multipronged approach that honors Black people across the country regardless of socioeconomic background and personal identity. What the Black [POLICY] Agenda will demand is that stakeholders are compelled enough to challenge existing systems that continue to undermine the lives of Black people in this country. In the final chapter of *The Black Agenda*, readers will hear from:

- **Cliff Albright,** cofounder of Black Voters Matter, a grassroots organization that worked to bring millions of Black voters to the polls during the 2020 presidential election as well as the Georgia runoff election. His essay illustrates the damage of voter suppression and how policy makers in Washington, D.C., can be instrumental in delivering sustained voter protections to Black voters.

- Economist **Dania V. Francis** emphasizes the need for Black policy wonks and legislative staff to be on the frontlines of the twenty-first-century civil rights movement in addition to activists and organizers.

- Senior advisor of the U.S. Department of Agriculture **Olugbenga Ajilore** discusses how the future of justice-centered policies begins with the Black rural South and why ignoring them is no longer something the country can afford.

- Economist **William "Sandy" Darity Jr.** makes the case for a twenty-first-century Economic Bill of Rights, which is a universal benefits package for all American citizens that ranges from free access to the internet to a federal job guarantee. Additionally, Darity suggests reparations for African Americans as one way to address the racial wealth gap.

BLACK VOTERS (ALWAYS) MATTER: VOTING RIGHTS IN THE TWENTY-FIRST CENTURY

Cliff Albright

Voting rights have always been a critical component of Black America's struggle for true freedom, justice, and improved quality of life. But our long history of fighting for voting rights, punctuated by the current onslaught of voter suppression efforts, demonstrates two points: first, securing our voting rights is going to take a level of direct action and civil disobedience we have not seen on voting issues since the 1960s; and second, the targets of our actions will need to be our apparent allies just as much as our known opposition, if not more so.

Even during the era of slavery, free Black people in the Northern states cherished the right to vote, but had to navigate Northern racism to protect those rights. In 1790, most Northern states actually allowed Black men to vote (Maryland, Massachusetts, New York, Pennsylvania, and Vermont) as well as North Carolina. However, as the years progressed, several states, including those newly added to the Union, implemented Black Codes to deny free Black people the right to vote. By the time the Civil War ended, nineteen of twenty-four Northern states did not allow Black people to vote.

For a variety of reasons, including the failures of a U.S. education system, which has never taught anything resembling a critical race theory, most Americans do not know that Black (male) voting rights were originally granted *not* in 1965 but in 1870 via the Fifteenth Amendment. And among those who know about the Fifteenth Amendment, even fewer understand the struggles that led to the amendment passing and the role that Black people played in demanding those voting rights.

For decades, free Black people in Northern states used a variety of mechanisms to express their desires and demands for voting rights, including a series of national gatherings known as (National) Colored Conventions, which took place beginning in 1830. At the 1864 convention, over which Frederick Douglass presided, the participants approved a statement that declared the following about voting rights:

> We are asked, even by some Abolitionists, why we cannot be satisfied, for the present at least, with personal freedom . . . The possession of that [voting] right is the keystone to the arch of human liberty: and, without that, the whole may at any moment fall to the ground . . . If you still ask why we want to vote, we answer, Because we don't want to be mobbed from our work, or insulted with impunity at every corner. We are men, and want to be as free in our native country as other men.

Our demands eventually led to the Fifteenth Amendment guarantee of voting rights, but the promise of that amendment was short-lived as the Reconstruction era was ended by the 1877 Tilden-Hayes Compromise. "Radical" Republicans, our allies at the time, who had promoted Black voting rights, were given the presidency as Black civil rights were crushed under the weight of Jim Crow segregation and white terrorism for decades. Even after white women obtained the right to vote through the Nineteenth Amendment, Black women were still denied voting rights in spite of the vital contributions they made to the suffragist movement.

Such would remain the case until the civil rights movement, or what some call the second Reconstruction. Although the voting rights movement actually took place over decades, it was largely the intense two years of the Mississippi Freedom Summer of 1964 and Selma in 1965 that caught the nation's attention. In particular, after President Lyndon B. Johnson had repeatedly told movement leaders that it was not the appropriate time for the Voting Rights Act, it was Selma's Bloody Sunday that forced him into action. As in the 1800s, our direct actions as Black people, and demands of our supporters, made the difference.

Fast-forward to today and the onslaught of voter suppression bills we have seen since the historic November 2020 election. According to the Brennan Center, "more than 400 bills with provisions that restrict voting access have been introduced in 49 states in the 2021 legislative sessions." At the time of this writing, at least eighteen states have enacted thirty laws that restrict access to the vote. The bills, exclusively proposed by state legislatures controlled by the Republican Party, are part of the white backlash in response to historic Black voter turnout, not only in the presidential election but in the January 2021 runoff election for two U.S. Senate seats in Georgia.

There are two pieces of legislation that would go a long way toward stopping these voter suppression efforts. One of these, which would restore critical powers that the Supreme Court previously stripped from the 1965 Voting Rights Act and is also still in development, is appropriately named after civil rights icon John Lewis. The other bill, the For the People Act, which would create new election standards and expand voting access, has already been passed by the House of Representatives and is waiting for action in the Senate as of August 2021. Unfortunately, Senate Republicans are using a process known as the filibuster to prevent a vote on this important bill, which a majority of Americans support.

Nevertheless, the fact of the matter is that because of the November 2020 election, Democrats do not just have control of the White House and the House of Representatives but also control of the Senate via a 50–50 tie and the tie-breaking vote by Vice President Kamala Harris. Democrats have the power to end the filibuster and pass the legislation necessary to protect and restore Black voting rights, and the reason they have that power is because Black voters turned out. Black voters helped President Joe Biden win his Democratic nomination, won him the presidency, and then provided him the votes to bring in two Georgia senators necessary to enable him to govern.

Black folks are yet again in the position of having to protest for our voting rights. And once again, much like our white abolitionist allies of the 1800s, and white allies during the 1960s, including President Johnson, it is the people who are theoretically "on our side"—people who in a real sense are in fact indebted to us—whom we must push into action. Indeed, it is a pattern that Dr. King warned us all about in his 1963 *Letter from Birmingham Jail,* in which he expressed his grave disappointment with the white moderate, whom he almost viewed to be as much of an obstacle as the white supremacists. Dr. King addressed white supporters—particularly faith leaders—who claimed to support the objectives of the movement but not the tactics or timing of civil disobedience.

Among other things, Dr. King explained how those who do not experience the daily indignities and impact of racism are often content to suggest waiting and how that often translates into "never."

And so here we are, in 2021, with a president who says he wants to "heal the soul of the nation." You cannot heal the soul of the nation, however, when you are fundamentally unclear about how cancerous that soul has become or, perhaps more importantly, if you are in denial about how long the cancer has been present, and from whence it came.

The current battle is going to take more than phone calls, text messages, and social media posts. It is going to require sustained direct action, including civil disobedience. That is why my organization, Black Voters Matter, which I cofounded with Ms. LaTosha Brown, along with dozens of other national, state, and local partner organizations, organized a Freedom Ride for Voting Rights that made stops and held rallies in eighteen cities in ten states over a nine-day period—to inform and inspire people to match the commitment of Freedom Riders from sixty years ago. That is why the Poor People's Campaign is conducting weekly civil disobedience actions. Their campaign has already seen over one hundred activists arrested. That is why the Black Women's Roundtable organized an action, which led to the arrest of the sitting chairperson of the Congressional Black Caucus, Congresswoman Joyce Beatty of Ohio.

Part of the hope for these types of actions is to inspire other members of Congress to see that at this moment their role must go beyond passing legislation and must include joining with activists on such actions. One week later, Congressman Hank Johnson answered the call, as he, eight activists, and I were arrested at the Senate office building as we chanted, "Hey hey! Ho ho! The filibuster has got to go!" The truth is that there should not be this much difficulty and resistance toward protecting one of our most basic rights. We should not have to fight so hard, at times risking life and liberty, and facing similar barriers that our ancestors faced over two hundred years ago. It is not a burden we should have to bear, but like those who came before us, it is one that we will take on.

With that said, we must face a stark reality. As a professor once said to me: any time you are a minority group in a majority-rule system, you've got a fundamental problem. We must extend the conversation beyond just voting rights and address how the structure of governance impacts our voting power. When the 1993 nomination of Lani Guinier to head the civil rights division of the Justice Department was withdrawn, the concept of proportional representation did not receive the debate that the Black community needed to take place. The recent June 2021 reintroduction of the Fair Representation Act in Congress could help generate a long overdue discussion.

In the meantime, Black Voters have always mattered—then, now, and forever; and as we always say at Black Voters Matter, "Can't stop, won't stop!"

Works Cited

"New SPLC Poll: Two-Thirds of Voters Support Passage of 'For the People Act.'" Southern Poverty Law Center, May 6, 2021. https://www.splcenter.org/news/2021/05/06/new-splc-poll-two-thirds-voters-support-passage-people-act.

"Proceedings of the National Convention of Colored Men; Held in the City of Syracuse, N.Y.; October 4, 5, 6, and 7, 1864; with the Bill of Wrongs and Rights; and the Address to the American People." Colored Conventions Project. https://omeka.coloredconventions.org/items/show/282.

"67 Percent of Americans Support H.R.1 For the People ACT." Data for Progress, January 22, 2021. https://www.dataforprogress.org/blog/2021/1/22/majority-support-hr1-democracy-reforms.

"Voting Laws Roundup: July 2021." Brennan Center, July 22, 2021. https://www.brennancenter.org/our-work/research-reports/voting-laws-roundup-july-2021.

THE NEXT CIVIL RIGHTS
MOVEMENT REQUIRES POLICY WONKS

Dania V. Francis

In the run-up to and the immediate aftermath of the 2016 presidential election, America bore witness to the exposure of the myth of post-racialism. The euphoria of the election and reelection of President Barack Obama had many Americans convinced that the country had finally transcended its shameful racial history. Explicit racial bias, we were to believe, had been successfully pushed out of the mainstream and into the crackpot fringes of white supremacist groups. Those of us who work with and live in America's racial realities, however, knew better.

During his presidency, Donald Trump made numerous statements overtly hostile to Blacks, Hispanics, Muslims, and women, among others. His open intimidation toward these historically, and currently, marginalized groups emboldened hate groups and their accompanying ideologies.

While the prospect of white supremacist ideology emerging from the shadows and being granted mainstream legitimacy is a grave concern, the bigger threat to the social, political, and economic well-being of the marginalized is in fact the ability of those in power to surreptitiously craft harmful and discriminatory outcomes from *seemingly* race-neutral policies and legislation.

As the nation moves forward from the damaging years of the Trump presidency, there will be aspects of the administration's policy agenda that will get lots of media attention and cause much uproar among advocates for the marginalized. These policies will be easy targets for reversal and correction. But the hidden danger will be in the parts of his agenda that slide under the radar and cause long-lasting harm to marginalized communities.

What we really need now in the battle for civil rights are policy wonks and legislative specialists who will be the first line of defense against the proliferation of surreptitiously discriminatory legislation. Oftentimes, federal, state, and local legislative proposals may be hundreds of pages long. Within those hundreds of pages, there may be only one or two pages, or even one or two sentences, that have been crafted to the benefit of a white, male, powerful elite at the expense of the marginalized masses. We need trained policy experts who can unearth these obscure lines of policy and bring to light the way bias and discrimination are institutionally codified.

There is a long history of this type of discriminatory policy formation in the United States. Southern Black citizens in the post-Reconstruction era were disenfranchised through the implementation of poll taxes and literacy tests as a barrier to voter registration. On their face, the restrictions appear to be race neutral since they also applied to white citizens. However, the introduction of grandfather clauses—which exempted citizens from these voting barriers if their ancestors had the right to vote prior to the Civil War—effectively restricted the vote from most Black Southerners while grandfathering in poorer white Southerners who might otherwise have had trouble meeting the voting requirements.

The unprecedented voter turnout in the 2020 elections that secured Joe Biden's presidential win and Democratic control of the Senate has and will undoubtedly spur a twenty-first-century campaign of voter suppression by Republicans at all levels of government. Some of the legislation they will likely propose will be transparent attempts to suppress minority votes. There is also the possibility, however, that Republican lawmakers will propose voting legislation that is seemingly practical and race-neutral. Minoritized communities will need legislative and policy experts to expose these suppressive attempts for what they are.

As the country attempts to recover from the devastating personal and economic consequences of the COVID-19 pandemic, lawmakers will be called upon to pass legislation that strengthens social safety nets and gets the economy back on track. If history is any example, however, Black Americans are in danger of being disproportionately excluded from the benefits of a large economic stimulus and relief package.

The New Deal, the Fair Deal, and the GI Bill were gargantuan pieces of American legislative history that involved a Faustian bargain with Southern political elites that was struck to provide relief from the Great Depression and a Post–World War II path to prosperity for the majority of Americans at the exclusion of Black Americans and other marginalized groups.

Southerners lobbied to exclude domestic and farm laborers from receiving benefits (65 percent of Black workers were employed as domestic or farm laborers at the time) and to designate the management of the newly created benefits programs to state and local administrators. This excluded many Southern Blacks who lived under the state-sanctioned second-class citizenship wrought by Jim Crow laws. Over 60 percent of Black Americans still lived in the South through the 1950s.

The implementation of these benefits programs ultimately worked to disproportionately exclude Black Americans from participation in the social welfare policies that effectively created the American middle class. Although many of these state-sanctioned legislative restrictions and discriminatory policies were phased out through the 1950s, 1960s, and 1970s, their cumulative effects—enduring residential and school segregation, and widening racial wealth disparities—persist today. And to guard against the exclusion of Black Americans from the COVID-19 relief and recovery efforts, we need policy wonks and legislative experts to comb through proposed legislation and amendments line by line to bring to light provisions that will create disproportionate disadvantages.

The Paycheck Protection Program implemented in 2020 to help support businesses affected by the pandemic benefited larger companies in wealthier areas, leaving low-income, minority communities to fend for themselves. The provisions of the law that allowed large banks—that have a history of excluding Black Americans—to act as intermediaries in applying for and dispersing the funds should have raised immediate red flags for policy experts concerned with equity. Drawing more attention to that aspect of the legislation may have created political pressure to consider a more equitable distribution mechanism.

Unless we are able to expose the discriminatory policies that pose as race-neutral legislation, minoritized communities will continue to be gaslighted and scapegoated by those who would blame them for racial disparities in economic, social, and political life. Shining a light on this particular form of institutional bias will help chip away at deficit-based explanations for racial disparities and shift the focus toward eliminating structural barriers faced by racial minorities.

The need for policy wonks as legislative experts is clear. Their focus should be singular—comb through legislation at all levels of government and shine a light on discriminatory policies. As such, they must not be distracted by the sideshow of physical racial hostility and intimidation that became hallmarks of the Trump administration. Groups like the ACLU and the Southern Poverty Law Center, among others, can continue to address those hate groups. Instead, the chosen policy and legislative experts should remain laser focused, as history has demonstrated the potential for state-sponsored policy to create much more widespread and persistent damage than any single hate group.

Works Cited

Hopkins, Jamie Smith, Taylor Johnston, and Pratheek Rebala. "PPP Loans Were Supposed to Prioritize Low-Income Areas During the Pandemic. They Didn't." Center for Public Integrity, December 11, 2020. https://publicintegrity.org/inequality-poverty-opportunity/covid-divide/ppp-loans-did-not-prioritize-low-income-areas-small-businesses-pandemic/.

Katznelson, Ira. *When Affirmative Action Was White: An Untold History of Racial Inequality in Twentieth-Century America.* New York: W. W. Norton, 2005.

THE BLACK BELT: AMERICA'S BLACK RURAL SOUTH

Olugbenga Ajilore

I n American public discourse about African American communities, the focus is almost entirely on urban residents. Yet a significant population of African Americans live in rural America, flyover states that are typically ignored by policy makers.

Racism in the labor market drove the Great Migration of African Americans to the North during the first part of the twentieth century. While millions of African Americans left Southern towns for larger cities in the North, such as New York, Chicago, Detroit, and Milwaukee, and on the West Coast, such as Los Angeles, Oakland, and Seattle, there has been a return of African Americans back to Southern states over the past forty years, due to ongoing civil rights successes along with kinship ties.

While the racism in the Southern labor market is not equivalent to that of the Jim Crow era, it still permeates the region and can explain the continued lack of economic mobility, especially in rural areas. Defining this Black Belt as the set of counties in the South with an African American population over 40 percent, data show that this region falls behind in several economic indicators. In the Black Belt, residents experience a persistent poverty rate, defined as poverty over 10 percent over several decades, of 11.6 percent versus the overall rate of 6.3 percent in the United States. Median income in the Black Belt is $38,000 versus $62,000 in the United States. And in 2019, the unemployment rate in the Black Belt was 5.27 percent versus 3.7 percent overall in the United States. The inequities laid bare in these indicators are indeed the outcome of structural racism.

To understand how these indicators came to be, look no further than right-to-work laws that served to limit mobility through the labor market for low-income and African American households during the early part of the twentieth century. Right-to-work laws are statewide ordinances that make it illegal for workers and employers to negotiate contracts that require beneficiaries to pay their fair share of administration costs. Many of the Southern states enacted these laws during the late forties and early fifties, during the height of the civil rights movement. Collective bargaining rights have been shown to be very important in closing earnings gaps and providing pathways for upward mobility for African Americans. Recent analysis has shown the wages are lower for African Americans in right-to-work states than in states without right-to-work laws.

The historical sanctioning of racist labor policy along with structural racism in other parts of the economy have maintained the dismal economic prospects for African Americans in the rural Southern region, but there are several intentional policies that can begin to reverse these outcomes.

First, providing a significant investment in public services designed to help low-income households is essential. Many Southern states have not expanded Medicaid, a provision of the Affordable Care Act, which limited health care access for their residents and diminished the financial viability of rural hospitals. The lack of health care has been a huge problem for Black residents in the rural South as the virus ravaged many of their communities. Not only are residents of the Black Belt more susceptible to contracting the virus, Black residents had a higher death rate from COVID than most other groups.

However, public service provision is not just about health care but also about the insufficient level and quality of basic public infrastructure. Through racist zoning laws, deed restrictions, explicit discrimination, and other forms of housing segregation, Black communities have evolved into neighborhoods plagued by pollution, leading to the many health inequities we see now. The cumulative and deadly impacts of having sources of pollution concentrated in communities of color have led to the health inequities that are further amplified by the ongoing pandemic. Infrastructure investment in sustainable solutions to reduce pollution and support clean and healthy communities is critical moving forward.

Second, we must strengthen worker power through boosting unionization, ensuring collective bargaining rights, and implementing wage boards across a variety of industries. Wage boards are governing councils composed of worker representatives, community organizations, and policy makers that set minimum wage and worker standards in a given industry. Repealing right-to-work laws, raising the minimum wage past the federal level of just $7.25, and ensuring the Occupational Safety and Health Administration enforces existing employment law are all necessary steps toward boosting earnings for all households, particularly African American households, and ensuring economic mobility.

The minimum wage has been key in the narrowing racial income gaps, particularly in 1967, when the wages were not only raised but also expanded to more people. It is also time to repeal Section 14(c) of the Fair Labor Standards Act (FLSA) that permits disabled workers to be paid a subminimum wage and results in a majority of these workers being employed in segregated settings. Tipped workers, who are disproportionately workers of color, are also still relegated to receiving the subminimum wage of $2.13.

Third, we must combat structural racism in the criminal justice system. This is not a call for simple policy but rather a suite of serious reforms that may take decades to implement. We must engage in criminal justice reform by removing punitive laws and reducing sentencing policies that are selectively enforced. We must also engage in reform that assists returning citizens, so they are able to access programs for the promotion of economic mobility.

To be able to fully tackle criminal justice reform, we must reimagine public safety in a form that supports communities and their residents. There are two mechanisms by which reimagining public safety can benefit communities and create jobs. First, involvement in the justice system creates barriers to employment for many people, especially African Americans. If people do not enter the system, they will end up on a higher employment trajectory and therefore contribute to a more resilient economy. This includes the removal of school resource officers who provide a direct pathway from schools to the carceral system. Second, shifting resources toward other services like education and mental health will strengthen communities by providing employment opportunities for those within the community and creating stronger ties and bonds among the residents.

In many ways, the set of counties that represent the fertile

soil that has driven the Southern economy and political economy for generations is a bellwether for the path this country
has followed for hundreds of years. These counties represent the
region that developed cotton, which was harvested by African
slaves until their emancipation in 1865. Then these crops were
harvested by the overwhelmingly Black sharecroppers who were
denied basic rights and freedoms until the civil rights movements during the middle of the twentieth century. State and
federal policy makers have continued to disenfranchise the
population from then till now.

At the end of the day, while the residents and citizens of the
rural Black South have disproportionately felt the sting of this
pandemic, the path for our country toward a robust, dynamic,
and inclusive recovery also begins with the Black Belt.

AFRICAN AMERICAN REPARATIONS AND AN ECONOMIC BILL OF RIGHTS FOR THE TWENTY-FIRST CENTURY

William "Sandy" Darity Jr.

The Black-white wealth disparity effectively captures the economic impact of the full trajectory of racial injustice in American society from slavery to the present moment. You can see this disparity manifest in health care and jobs, especially in the aftermath of the COVID-19 pandemic. On the one hand, Black employment has been disproportionately concentrated in jobs that require personal services and personal contact. This has meant many jobs deemed nonessential vanished during the course of the pandemic, costing Black workers employment and income. On the other hand, Blacks who have kept their jobs have been put at risk for greater exposure to the coronavirus. For example, Black workers are about 30 percent of transportation workers, 22 percent of animal slaughtering and processing workers, and about 25 percent of health care and hospital services providers. As economist Rhonda Vonshay Sharpe notes, jobs held by Black workers frequently may be designated essential, but the people performing the jobs are treated as disposable.

Given the grave and devastating impact of the COVID-19 crisis, we need to adopt an Economic Bill of Rights for the

Twenty-First Century for all Americans and implement a robust reparations plan for Black American descendants of slavery in the United States. Even in the absence of a pandemic, the nation would be a better society—more just and equitable—if it enacts both of these policies. Adoption of these policies today places within our power the capacity to create the Great Republic.

An Economic Bill of Rights is a program of universal benefits guaranteed to all Americans as a birthright. Inspired by Franklin Roosevelt's proposed Second Bill of Rights, the Economic Bill of Rights for the Twenty-First Century promises to give all citizens a guarantee of a decent standard of living and a reasonable opportunity to participate in the nation's social and political life. Highlighted here are four elements of the Economic Bill of Rights for the Twenty-First Century: the federal job guarantee, national health insurance, public banking / postal banking, and universal access to Wi-Fi.

A federal job guarantee is a right to public sector employment for all adults at non-poverty wages, with benefits similar to those received by all federal civil servants. If such a program had been in place prior to the pandemic, there would have been an existing public payroll that would have been easy to move people onto who have lost jobs. Moreover, the federal government could have borne the expense of safety protocols to better maintain the public sector jobs. Artists and entertainers who no longer could tour or benefit from public gatherings could have been employed under the federal jobs program in a fashion similar to the Works Progress Administration in the 1930s. A federal jobs guarantee would also help restore a postal banking system to undercut predatory lending. In addition, federal jobs guarantee employees could contribute to the construction of the infrastructure for solarization to support a Green Economy.

A public banking/postal banking system would assure all Americans of public provision of low-cost customer deposit, savings, and credit services. While the Federal Reserve system is a public bank, it does not provide customer services. Most of its activities support private banking operations. A new system of public banking, including the mobilization of the postal service toward that end, can produce an infrastructure that will support small depositors and eliminate predatory lending.

A national health insurance program would establish access to medical care for all Americans. No one would be without coverage. The connection between having a job and having health insurance would be broken. Not only would the presence of national health insurance have been valuable in grappling with COVID-19, it would make possible greater preparedness in the event of recurrence of an emergency similar to the current one.

Free broadband services for everyone would mean universal access to the internet and to the machinery, such as laptops or cell phones, for making use of the internet. Wi-Fi for all would lift barriers to social interaction, particularly important in a period where classroom-based instruction has undergone disruption. It also would expand the possibilities for adults beyond the schooling years to work more safely on a remote basis, considering the impact the pandemic has had on the nature of work.

While the programs listed above will stand under a universal platform of economic rights for all Americans, elimination of the nation's glaring Black-white wealth disparity will require a race-specific plan for reparations. Did you know one-quarter of white households in the United States possess a net worth in excess of $1 million, while only 4 percent of Black households possess a similar level of wealth? Though African Americans whose ancestors were enslaved in the United States constitute 12 percent of the nation's population, they possess less than 2 percent of the nation's wealth. This small share corresponds to a condition where the average white household has a net worth $840,900 greater than the average Black household.

The immense expenditures made by the federal government in response, earlier, to the Great Recession and, recently, to the current health crisis demonstrate the feasibility of funding both an Economic Bill of Rights for the Twenty-First Century and African American reparations. The fact that the social justice agenda was not in place prior to COVID-19 does not mean it cannot be adopted now. The urgency of the moment must continue even when the pandemic comes to an end.

It has become a cliché to say every crisis creates an opportunity. In this case, the opportunity existed long before the crisis. If the crisis spurs the nation, finally, to embrace bold, transformative policies that shape a new future—the Great Republic—then the lessons learned from COVID-19 would have proved to be both tragic and hopeful in the fight for equality and equity.

Works Cited

Bassett, Mary T., and Sandro Galea. "Reparations as a Public Health Priority—A Strategy for Ending Black-White Wealth Disparities." *New England Journal of Medicine,* October 8, 2020. https://www.nejm.org/doi/full/10.1056/NEJMp2026170.

Chatterjee, Rhitu. "How the Pandemic is Widening the Racial Wealth Gap." SHOTS: Health News from NPR, September 18, 2020. https://www.npr.org/sections/health-shots/2020/09/18/912731744/how-the-pandemic-is-widening-the-racial-wealth-gap.

"The Color of Coronavirus: COVID-19 Deaths by Race and Ethnicity in the U.S." APM Research Lab, October 15, 2020. https://www.apmresearchlab.org/covid/deaths-by-race.

Darity, William, Jr., Fenaba R. Addo, and Imari Z. Smith. "A Subaltern Middle Class: The Case of the Missing 'Black Bourgeoisie' in America." *Contemporary Economic Policy,* 2020. https://socialequity.duke.edu/wp-content/uploads/2020/05/DarityAddoSmithCEP2020.pdf.

Darity, William, Jr., and A. Kirsten Mullen. "Coronavirus Is Making the Case for Reparations Clearer." *Newsweek,* May 5, 2020. https://www.newsweek.com/coronavirus-making-case-black-reparations-clearer-ever-opinion-1501887.

Paul, Mark V., William Darity Jr., and Darrick Hamilton. "An Economic Bill of Rights in the 21st Century." *American Prospect,* March 2018. https://www.researchgate.net/publication/323560574_An_Economic_Bill_of_Rights_for_the_21st_Century.

Sasso, Michael. "Black-Owned Firms Still Close at Double Whites' Rate in U.S." *Washington Post,* July 14, 2020. https://www.washingtonpost.com/business/on-small-business/black-owned

-firms-still-close-at-double-whites-rate-in-us/2020/07/14
/3e438492-c5dd-11ea-a825–8722004e4150_story.html.

Valdez, Purinima. "What Can I Do? A Call for Pediatric Providers to Engage in Antiracism and Social Justice for the Health of Their Patients." *Journal of Developmental and Behavioral Pediatrics* 41, no. 7 (2020): 504–505.

Wrigley-Field, Elizabeth. "US Racial Inequality May Be as Deadly as COVID-19." *Proceedings of the National Academy of Sciences (PNAS)* 117, no. 36 (2020): 21854–21856. https://www.pnas.org/content/117/36/21854.short.

ACKNOWLEDGMENTS

First and foremost, I would like to thank God for providing me with an opportunity to be a conduit for these incredible voices within the Black community. As a person who values dialogue and learning out loud, being able to provide others with an opportunity to engage in both is a responsibility I do not take lightly. As I write this, I recognize how blessed I am to be providing a platform for Black expertise that gets to live in libraries, bookstores, classrooms, businesses, and the like. While the book is not exhaustive, this first attempt at centering Black voices is significant and worth celebrating.

With that said, the real stars of *The Black Agenda* are those who willingly chose to share their viewpoints with the world in thoughtful and meaningful ways. These are the individuals that should be invited to speaking engagements, prime-time news slots, and podcasts. I would like to thank each contributor for daring to offer solutions that will likely be part of the conversation for decades to come and offering encouragement and affirmation when needed. Your words are what will push forward the next iteration of public discourse across these policy areas.

To Dr. Tressie McMillan Cottom, whose words resonate throughout the foreword and in life, thank you for not just being my blueprint for public intellectualism but also agreeing to usher in the essays of this book. Additionally, thank you to *New York Times* bestselling authors Wes Moore and Chelsea

Clinton, who recognized, early, what a book like this could become. Wes aptly saying to me that "this book will change the trajectory of my life" and Chelsea affirming the long-standing value of a body of work like this further confirmed to me the importance of this project. Thank you as well to every person who received an early preview of the book and offered their support.

I would like to also offer huge thanks to my wonderful literary team: my agent, Leila Campoli, who believed in the mere mention of the idea before it materialized and made space for me to be my fullest self; my editors, Hannah O'Grady and Laura Clark, who saw the vision and helped bring it to life through many drafts and edits; the St. Martin's Press publishing and marketing teams that bet on a then twenty-four-year-old emerging voice who is still very much adjusting to any kind of spotlight; and the wonderful Danielle Horton and Haleemat Adekoya, who helped make the entire process of writing, editing, and putting together a book possible. I am deeply grateful for each of you.

And finally, I would like to show love to the wonderful communities that have helped me become the woman I am today. This includes my support system, who grounds me and keeps me humble; academic and professional spaces that empower me to discover and lean into my strengths; and all the readers who decide to pick up this book. Thank you for making the decision to learn alongside me.

The truth is I have absolutely no idea what comes next, but what I do know is that *The Black Agenda* offers several places to start and tens of people to learn from. The book provides the kind of hope one experiences in the midst of a successful movement or right after hearing "The Hill We Climb" from the indomitable Amanda Gorman.

If even an ounce of what is shared in these pages is considered and implemented, I know that our country, our world, in the present and in the future, will be better off. So, here's to progress—may it come soon.

ABOUT THE CONTRIBUTORS

Climate

Dr. Marshall Shepherd is the Georgia Athletic Association Distinguished Professor of Geography and Atmospheric Sciences at the University of Georgia and director of its Atmospheric Sciences Program. Prior to academia, he spent twelve years as a scientist at NASA's Goddard Space Flight Center. Dr. Shepherd is the host of the Weather Channel's *Weather Geeks* podcast and a senior contributor to *Forbes* magazine. In 2021, Dr. Shepherd was elected to the National Academy of Sciences, National Academy of Engineering, and the American Academy of Arts and Sciences and has received numerous other awards. He received his BS, MS, and Ph.D. in meteorology from Florida State University.

Abigail Abhaer Adekunbi Thomas is an environmentalist and climate justice advocate. Hailing from Ethiopia and Nigeria and having lived in over five countries, she has been exposed to the disproportionate impacts of climate change in low-income countries from a young age. She has worked as an African Union advisor on climate change initiatives and served as a council member to the resource hub Intersectional Environmentalist. She is currently a member of the World Economic Forum's global youth hub for #GenerationRestoration and works on environmental employee engagement at the outdoor gear and apparel company Patagonia.

Her experiences working across global environmental issues has led her to develop a relentless passion to advocate for environmental and climate justice globally.

Mary Annaïse Heglar is a writer, editor, teacher, and the cocreator and cohost of *Hot Take.* In 2020, she joined Columbia University's writer-in-residence program, a joint initiative between Columbia University's Earth Institute and the Natural Resources Defense Council (NRDC). Additionally, she contributed an essay to *All We Can Save,* edited by Drs. Ayana Elizabeth Johnson and Katharine K. Wilkinson.

arii lynton-smith has a BA in cultural nonprofit administration (concentrations in anthropology, human geography, Pan-African studies and nonprofit studies) from the University of Louisville. they facilitate and teach courses with college students and community centers. arii is a freelance writer and digital media manager. they focus their work on practicing the world in which they envision that actively supports QTBIPOC. In 2020, arii launched their mutual aid project apothecarii, where they sell herbal medicine on a pay-what-you-can basis. they are also a member of Aflorar Herb Collective, an herbal mutual-aid network that provides herbal medicine to organizers and activists across the country.

Health Care

Dr. Dara D. Mendez, MPH, is faculty in the Department of Epidemiology and interim director of the Center for Health Equity at the University of Pittsburgh Graduate School of Public Health. Mendez is a national expert who applies a variety of methods and approaches in her work related to the complex intersections between racism, multiple forms of oppression, stress, and place in understanding Black maternal and infant health as well as racial/ ethnic inequities in pregnancy, birth, and women's health. She is a founding member of the Pennsylvania Maternal Mortality Review Committee, former board chair of the National Women's Health Network, and executive member of the Black Equity Coalition in Pittsburgh, Pennsylvania.

Dr. Jewel Scott is a nurse with nearly two decades of experience in community-based primary care. Her nursing background led to her research on preventing hypertension and heart disease among young Black women. Her research aims to change the narrative around Black women's health, moving away from blaming those with chronic disease to understanding the influence of social structures and systems on health and identifying protective factors. She is currently developing projects examining the relationships between racism, mental health, and blood pressure among childbearing people. Dr. Scott is a National Institutes of Health (NIH) funded researcher and an RWJF Future of Nursing Scholar.

At the University of California San Francisco, **Dr. Monica McLemore** is a tenured associate professor in the Family Health Care Nursing Department and an affiliated scientist with Advancing New Standards in Reproductive Health. Her program of research is focused on understanding reproductive health and justice. To date, she has eighty-two peer-reviewed articles, op-eds, and commentaries, and her research has been cited in three amicus briefs to the Supreme Court of the United States, two National Academies of Science, Engineering, and Medicine reports, and a data visualization project in the 2019 Future of Medicine edition of *Scientific American.*

Dr. Yolonda Yvette Wilson is associate professor of health care ethics at Saint Louis University, with additional appointments in the Departments of Philosophy and African American Studies. She earned a Ph.D. in philosophy from the University of North Carolina at Chapel Hill. She is currently working on a monograph, *Black Death: Racial Justice, Priority-Setting, and Care at the End of Life.* Professor Wilson's public scholarship on issues at the intersection of bioethics, race, and gender has appeared in the Hastings Center's Bioethics Forum, *USA Today,* and the Conversation and republished in outlets such as the *Los Angeles Times,* the *Chicago Tribune,* Salon.com, and the *Philly Voice.*

Wellness

Dr. Jaime Slaughter-Acey is a maternal and child health (MCH) and social epidemiologist whose work focuses on socio-environmental and psychosocial determinants of women's and family health across the life course, with emphasis on health equity. Her current research, funded by the Russell Sage Foundation and the National Institutes of Health (NIH), investigates the social significance of skin color as a driver of pre-pregnancy cardiometabolic health and birth outcomes for Black women. She is the principal investigator of the Interdisciplinary Research Invested in Social Equity (I-RISE) Collaboratory, which aims to integrate social science literature with epidemiologic and system science methods to the study of systemic racism, both structural and cultural, and its intersection with other aspects of social identity to create health and health care inequalities in MCH.

Tinu Abayomi-Paul is a writer and a disabled entrepreneur who provides coaching services to other microbusiness owners. After twenty years as an entrepreneur, eighteen as a well-known marketing and Google expert, Tinu had an awakening. After being diagnosed with cancer, she had to take almost three years off building her business, due to having several chronic diseases prior to the cancer, which complicated her recovery. Once safely on the other side, she realized other entrepreneurs, disabled and otherwise, could use the resources she developed to restart her life after cancer.

Dr. Jevay Grooms is an assistant professor with the Department of Economics at Howard University. Her research lies at the intersection of public economics, health economics, and studies of poverty and inequality. Her overall research agenda is to study the impediments to adequate health care delivery and health outcomes of underserved and vulnerable populations, with a keen intent to understand how poverty and the legacy of wealth inequality have contributed to health disparities among racial and ethnic minorities. Some of her current research focuses on domestic health policies and interventions geared toward individuals who suffer from substance use disorders and mental illness.

Ashlee Wisdom is the cofounder & CEO of Health In Her HUE, a digital platform that connects Black women and women of color to culturally sensitive health care providers, health content, and community. Health In Her HUE's mission is to reduce racial health disparities by leveraging the power of technology, media, and community to improve health outcomes for Black women. Wisdom is a champion for health equity and is passionate about centering equity in health care innovation. She received her BS from Howard University and a master of public health with a concentration in health care policy and management from New York University.

Education

Dr. Carycruz Bueno is an assistant professor of economics at Wesleyan University. She is an applied microeconomist who studies how education policy can eradicate education inequality. Her research addresses topics such as virtual schools, school choice, teacher labor markets, and student noncognitive skills. Her research interest stems from her experience as a special education teacher. She has received funding from the National Science Foundation, ASHE, and the National Economics Association. In 2021, she was named an Emerging Education Policy Scholar by the Thomas B. Fordham Institute. Prior to joining Wesleyan University, she was a postdoctoral researcher at Brown University. Dr. Bueno has been featured in *The Atlantic,* NPR's *Planet Money,* Bloomberg, and *Politico Nightly.*

Dr. Cruz Caridad Bueno is an economist specializing in economic development, gender violence, and the political economy of race, gender, and class inequality. She is an assistant professor of Black studies and the recipient of the 2014 Rhonda Williams Prize from the International Association for Feminist Economics for her qualitative research on low-income Black women workers—work funded by the Inter-American Foundation's Grassroots Development Fellowship—in the Dominican Republic and her quantitative research on the economic, political, and social correlates of gender violence. She is currently an assistant professor of Black studies at the State University of New York–New Paltz.

Dr. Lauren Christine Mims is an assistant professor in the Department of Educational Psychology at Ball State University. She holds a doctoral degree in educational psychology from the University of Virginia, a master's degree in child development from Tufts University, and a bachelor's degree from the University of Virginia. She was also appointed assistant director of the White House Initiative on Educational Excellence for African Americans during the Obama administration.

Dr. S. Mia Obiwo is an assistant professor of early childhood education at the University of Memphis. Her professional work and scholarship focus on critical issues in urban elementary schools and teacher education. Dr. Obiwo is committed to helping educators become culturally responsive, equity-oriented change agents in their classrooms and communities. She subscribes to the sociocultural principles of reciprocal teaching and learning experiences, and she believes that teachers must develop sociopolitical awareness that allows them to critique the existing cultural norms, patterns in behavior, and institutions that produce and maintain social inequities in schools and beyond. Dr. Obiwo has published work in the *Peabody Journal of Education* and the journal of School-University Partnerships.

Dr. Francheska Starks is a former public-school teacher with experience teaching students in grades K-12. She is currently an instructor at the University of West Georgia and her research focuses on the implications of social inequities on Black women and educators more broadly. She earned her doctorate in education from Georgia State University.

Dr. Kristen Broady is a fellow with the Metropolitan Policy Program at the Brookings Institution. She earned a BA in criminal justice at Alcorn State University and an MBA and Ph.D. in business administration with a major in economics at Jackson State

University. Dr. Broady is a member of Alpha Kappa Alpha Sorority Inc., and the Baltimore, Maryland, chapter of the Links Inc.

Dr. Fenaba R. Addo is an associate professor of public policy. Her recent work examines debt and wealth inequality with a focus on family and relationships and higher education, and union formation and economic strain as a social determinant of health and well-being. Widely published in academic journals and policy outlets, her work on racial disparities in student debt, older Black women and wealth, and the millennial racial wealth gap reflects her interests in bridging social demography with economic inequality and sheds light on the ways that societal inequalities stem from historical legacies of racial exclusion and discrimination, and how they get reproduced over time. She received her Ph.D. in policy analysis and management from Cornell University and holds a BS in economics from Duke University.

Technology

Deborah Raji is a Nigerian Canadian computer scientist and activist who works on algorithmic bias, AI accountability, and algorithmic auditing. Raji is currently a graduate student at the University of California, Berkeley. She has worked with Joy Buolamwini, Dr. Timnit Gebru, and the Algorithmic Justice League on researching gender and racial bias in facial recognition technology. She is an alum of Google's Ethical AI team and has been a research fellow at the Partnership on AI and AI Now Institute at New York University. Raji has been recognized by *MIT Technology Review* and Forbes 30 Under 30.

Dr. Brandeis Marshall is a data engineer, learning strategist, and entrepreneur who designs and delivers computing and data instruction for practical application for those aspiring, new, and experienced in the workforce. She started DataedX (pronounced data-ed-x). DataedX, at its core, counteracts automated oppression efforts with culturally responsive instruction and strategies. In 2019, she cocreated BeyondOne, DataedX's data prep online community for Black women, that provides a safe haven to grow, share, or pivot in data roles regardless of their profession. Marshall has taught as a professor at Spelman College and Purdue University. She received her bachelor's degree in computer science then received her Ph.D. from Rensselaer Polytechnic Institute in computer science in 2007.

Jordan Harrod is a Ph.D. candidate in medical engineering and medical physics at the Harvard-MIT Health Sciences and Technology program. Her research focuses on neurotechnology, arousal modulation, and machine learning, specifically using neuromodulation to understand pain and consciousness, and using neurotechnology and machine learning to develop new tools for brain stimulation. Outside of the lab, she creates videos about artificial intelligence on YouTube and TikTok as well as advocates for evidence-based policy.

Criminal Justice

Dr. Jamein P. Cunningham is an assistant professor at Cornell University's Department of Policy Analysis and Management and Economics. His teaching and research interests include labor economics, urban economics, economics of crime, and microeconometrics. Dr. Cunningham was a Ph.D. candidate in the Department of Economics and a Population Studies Center graduate trainee at the University of Michigan. He was a recipient of the Rackham Merit Fellowship and the Eunice Kennedy Shriver National Institute in Child Health and Development Fellowship. Before obtaining a Ph.D. at the University of Michigan, he completed his undergraduate degree at Michigan State University and received a master's degree in economics from the University of North Texas.

Tahir Anderson Duckett has spent fifteen years listening, advocating, and organizing in communities across the country. He is the executive director of a new academic center at Georgetown University Law Center focused on community safety. He recently practiced at Relman Colfax, a nationally renowned civil rights law firm, where he focused on discriminatory policing, housing, and education. He was also a founding executive committee member of Law for Black Lives–D.C., an organization providing legal and policy support to the Movement for Black Lives in the Washington, D.C., metropolitan area.

Dr. Hedwig "Hedy" Lee is a professor of sociology at Washington University in Saint Louis. She is also the codirector of the university's Center for the Study of Race, Ethnicity, and Equity. Hedy is broadly interested in the social determinants and consequences of population health and health disparities, with a particular focus on the role of structural racism in racial/ethnic health disparities. As an interdisciplinary scholar, Hedy has written articles spanning a range of topics and disciplines, including demography, medicine, political science, public health, social work, and sociology.

Preston Mitchum is a Black queer attorney, advocate, activist, and adjunct professor of law at Georgetown University Law Center. He has been featured in *The Washington Post,* BET.com, the Root, *The Atlantic,* BuzzFeed, CNN, and others. He was named a 2021

Rockwood Fellow for Leaders in Reproductive Health, Rights, and Justice and was named one of the 2020 Best LGBTQ Lawyers Under 40 by the LGBT Bar Association. Preston was the first openly LGBTQ chair of the Washington Bar Association Young Lawyers Division. He holds an LLM in law and government from American University Washington College of Law, a juris doctor from North Carolina Central University School of Law, and a BA in political science from Kent State University.

Economy

Dr. Karl Boulware is an assistant professor of economics at Wesleyan University. He is an applied macroeconomist who studies how macroeconomic policy can eradicate macroeconomic aspects of inequality. His recent research addresses topics such as the racial wealth stratification and the frequency of discrimination charges over the business cycle. Dr. Boulware's work has appeared in journals such as *Empirical Economics, Economics Letters, Economics Bulletin,* and *AEA Papers and Proceedings.* In his teaching, Professor Boulware specializes in quantitative methods, monetary economics, and financial markets.

Kyle K. Moore is an economist with the Economic Policy Institute's Program on Race, Ethnicity, and the Economy. He studies economic inequality in the frameworks of stratification economics, political economy, and public health. Prior to joining EPI, Moore was a senior policy analyst with the Joint Economic Committee's Democratic staff, where he authored reports on economic policy issues centered on race, class, age, and gender disparities. His research focuses on the intersection between racial economic disparities and health inequity across the life course, with particular focus on upstream structural causes of morbidity and mortality differences across race.

Angela Hanks is currently the chief legal counsel at the Department of Labor. Her previous role was as deputy executive director at Groundwork Collaborative, an economic policy nonprofit that works to advance an economic vision that delivers meaningful opportunity and prosperity for all. She previously worked as director of workforce development policy at the Center for American Progress and senior federal policy analyst at the National Skills Coalition. She also formerly worked for the Democratic staff of the House Oversight and Government Reform committee and was a legislative assistant to former U.S. representative Elijah Cummings (D-MD).

Janelle Jones was most recently the managing director for policy and research at Groundwork Collaborative. As part of the executive leadership team, she helped launch and build Groundwork. Before joining Groundwork in 2018, Janelle was an economic analyst at the Economic Policy Institute, working on a variety of labor market topics within EPI's Program on Race, Ethnicity, and the Economy. Currently, in her role as the chief economist for the U.S. Department of Labor, Janelle provides members of the Biden-Harris administration with expert advice and counsel regarding the economic impacts related to the department's work protecting and supporting America's workers, retirees, and their families.

Public Policy

Cliff Albright is the cofounder and executive director of Black Voters Matter Fund (BVM), which builds community and organizational capacity related to Black voting power. BVM was one of several organizations that mobilized Black voters to defeat Roy Moore in Alabama's 2017 U.S. Senate race and that has continued to mobilize Black voters throughout the South. Cliff hosts a weekly radio show in Atlanta, has served as an instructor of African American studies, and has contributed to *The New York Times, The Washington Post, The Guardian,* and others. Cliff previously lived in historic Selma, Alabama, where he focused on bringing financial resources to Alabama's Black Belt region. He incorporates a community-organizing perspective based on more than twenty years of social justice activism. Cliff attended Cornell University, where he obtained his BS in applied economics and an MPS in Africana studies. He also has an MBA from the University of Alabama.

Dr. Dania V. Francis is assistant professor of economics at UMass Boston. Her current research involves using experimental and quasi-experimental methods to identify structural causes of racial and socioeconomic academic achievement gaps. More broadly, Professor Francis's research interests include examining racial and socioeconomic disparities in education, wealth accumulation, and labor markets. Dr. Francis received her doctorate from Duke University and also holds a master's degree from Harvard University and a bachelor's degree from Smith College. She is a board member of the National Economic Association.

Dr. Olugbenga "Gbenga" Ajilore is a senior advisor in the Office of the Under Secretary for Rural Development at the United States Department of Agriculture. Formerly, Ajilore was a senior economist at the Center for American Progress, focused on macroeconomics, regional inequality, criminal justice, fiscal policy, race, and ethnicity. Ajilore was also previously an associate professor of economics at the University of Toledo. His work has been published in numerous journals, such as *The Review of Black Political*

Economy, Economics and Human Biology, the *Review of Economics of the Household,* and the *Atlantic Economic Journal.* Ajilore received his Ph.D. in economics from Claremont Graduate University in 2002. He earned his BA in applied mathematics and economics from the University of California, Berkeley, in 1996.

Dr. William A. "Sandy" Darity Jr. is the Samuel DuBois Cook Professor of Public Policy, African and African American Studies, and Economics and the director of the Samuel DuBois Cook Center on Social Equity at Duke University. He has served as chair of the Department of African and African American Studies and was the founding director of the Research Network on Racial and Ethnic Inequality at Duke. Darity's research focuses on inequality by race, class, and ethnicity, stratification economics, schooling and the racial achievement gap, North-South theories of trade and development, skin shade and labor market outcomes, the economics of reparations, the Atlantic slave trade and the Industrial Revolution, the history of economics, and the social psychological effects of exposure to unemployment. His most recent book, coauthored with A. Kirsten Mullen, is *From Here to Equality: Reparations for Black Americans in the Twenty-First Century* (2020).

RECOMMENDED READING

There are books that speak to the multifaceted nature of the Black experience in America in all areas of life that fill in the gaps *The Black Agenda* was unable to address fully. Here is a short list to begin your journey toward learning more:

- **Black Futures** by Jenna Wortham and Kimberly Drew

- **Hood Feminism** by Mikki Kendall

- **Thick: And Other Essays** by Tressie McMillan Cottom

- **Four Hundred Souls** by Keisha Blain and Ibram X. Kendi

- **All We Can Save** by Ayana Elizabeth Johnson and Katharine Wilkerson

- **Black AF History** by Michael Harriot

- **The Hill We Climb** by Amanda Gorman

- **The Memo** by Minda Harts

- **How the Word Is Passed** by Clint Smith III

- **The Sum of Us** by Heather McGhee

- **Caste** by Isabel Wilkerson

- **Ghosts in the Schoolyard: Racism and School Closings in Chicago's South Side** by Eve Ewing

- **The Intersectional Environmentalist** by Leah Thomas (coming March 2022)

- **How to Be an Antiracist** by Ibram X. Kendi

- **Race After Technology** by Ruha Benjamin

- **The Color of Money: Black Banks and the Racial Wealth Gap** by Mehrsa Baradaran

- **I'm Still Here: Black Dignity in a World Made for Whiteness** by Austin Channing Brown

- **A Black Women's History of the United States** by Daina Ramey Berry and Kali Nicole Gross

- **You Are Your Best Thing: Vulnerability, Shame Resilience, and the Black Experience** by Tarana Burke and Brené Brown

- **The Other Wes Moore** by Wes Moore

- **The 1619 Project** (book and *New York Times Magazine* series) by Nikole Hannah-Jones